Statue of Leif Eriksson in Reykjavik, Iceland

THE WORLD'S GREAT EXPLORERS

Leif Eriksson and the Vikings

By Charnan Simon

CHILDRENS PRESS®
CHICAGO

Viking Ships at Sea *by artist James G. Tyler*

Library of Congress Cataloging-in-Publication Data

Simon, Charnan.
Leif Eriksson and the Vikings / by Charnan Simon.
p. cm. — (The World's great explorers)
Includes bibliographical references and index.
Summary: Relates the adventures of the Norse explorer who left Greenland to sail west into uncharted waters in search of new land.
ISBN 0-516-03060-4
1. Leiv Eiriksson, d. ca. 1020—Juvenile literature. 2. Explorers—America—Biography—Juvenile literature. 3. Explorers—Norway—Biography—Juvenile literature. 4. America—Discovery and exploration—Norse—Juvenile literature. [1. Ericson, Leif, d. ca. 1020. 2. Explorers. 3. Vikings. 4. America—Discovery and exploration—Norse.] I. Title. II. Series.
E105.L47S56 1991
970.01'3'092—dc20 90-20804
[B] CIP
[92] AC

Project Editor: Ann Heinrichs
Designer: Lindaanne Donohoe
Cover Art: Steven Gaston Dobson
Engraver: Liberty Photoengraving

1 2 3 4 5 6 7 8 9 10 R 00 99 98 97 96 95 94 93 92 91

Leif Eriksson standing upon North American shores

Table of Contents

Chapter 1
Vinland the Good

The ship sailed out of the north. Its curved prow cut smoothly through the rough ocean waves. Atop its mast, a single square sail billowed in the wind. Slowly, steadily, the small ship pursued its southwesterly course.

On board the ship, thirty-five able seamen were busy tending their tackle and rigging. Up on the forward half-deck, their captain eagerly scanned the horizon for land. It had been nearly a week since Leif Eriksson had led his men from their homes in Greenland, an island in the Atlantic Ocean west of Norway. Surely they should sight land soon!

Leif Eriksson and his crew were Norsemen, Greenlanders of Norwegian descent. They had sailing bred into their blood and adventure into their bones. Now, in the year A.D. 1001, they were embarking on one of the greatest adventures of all time.

It had all begun the summer before. Leif Eriksson had just been presented to the court of Norway's King Olaf Tryggvason. When he returned to Greenland, the island was buzzing with talk of a man named Bjarni Herjolfsson—and of new lands Bjarni had sighted across the Western Ocean.

Bjarni Herjolfsson was a prosperous merchant whose ship traded between Norway and Iceland. (Iceland is an island that lies between Norway and Greenland; see map of Viking explorations on page 119.) It was Bjarni's habit to make trading voyages during the summer months. He spent his winters either in Norway or at his father's house in Iceland. But when Bjarni arrived at his father's home in the winter of 986, he found that the old man had moved to Greenland.

Bjarni was in a quandary. Greenland was a brand-new settlement in those days. Sailing there from Iceland was tricky at best and highly dangerous at worst. As one writer of the time put it: "Now there is [a] marvel in the seas of Greenland, the facts of which I do not know exactly. It is called 'sea hedges,' and it appears as if all the waves and tempests of the ocean have been collected into three heaps, out of which three billows have formed. These hedge in the entire sea, so that no opening can be seen anywhere; they are higher than lofty mountains and look like steep, overhanging cliffs. In only a few cases have men been known to escape when such a thing occurred."

But Bjarni was nothing if not stubborn. He had planned to winter at his father's house, and winter there he would. "I shall steer my ship for Greenland," he told his crew, "if you are prepared to go with me. Our voyage will seem fool-hardy, since none of us has ever sailed the Greenland Sea."

Bjarni's crew was an adventurous bunch, and they readily agreed to sail to Greenland. But three days out of port, they were swallowed up by dense fog and buffeting north winds. When the sun finally came out many days later, they had no idea where they were.

Bjarni Herjolfsson sights new lands in the North Atlantic.

Luckily, they spotted land in the distance. They drew near, but Bjarni frowned and shook his head. This hilly, forested shoreline didn't look like the Greenland he had heard about. He headed his ship back out to sea, sailing north until they had left the land behind.

Two days later, another shore was sighted. The crew looked questioningly at Bjarni, and again Bjarni shook his head. This flat, wooded country did not look like Greenland, either. "For," said Bjarni, "there are very big glaciers reported to be in Greenland."

By now the crew was growing impatient. They talked things over among themselves and agreed that it made sense to put ashore here, if only for fuel wood and water. But Bjarni disagreed. "You lack for neither," he said firmly, ignoring his men's grumbling.

Once again the crew hoisted sail and set out to sea. Three days later they sighted land for the third time. This was an island, high, mountainous, and glaciered. "This land looks good for nothing," pronounced Bjarni. His men didn't even bother to lower their sail.

Finally, after four more days of hard sailing, Bjarni and his men came upon a fourth land. "This looks very like what I was told about Greenland," said Bjarni, "and here we will make for the land."

This time they were in luck. The land was indeed Greenland, and Bjarni's father lived on the very cape where they anchored. After a long and perilous journey, Bjarni and his men had brought their ship safely to shore.

Bjarni spent the winter with his father, and the following spring he resumed his trading voyages. Fourteen years went by. Finally, around the year 1000, he returned to Greenland to live permanently with his father. Now retired, Bjarni spent many a long, cold Greenland winter evening recounting his tales of the strange new lands he had sighted in the west.

It was these tales that Leif Eriksson heard when he returned from King Olaf's court. It seemed that everyone in Greenland was marveling about what Bjarni had seen.

Leif marveled, too—at how Bjarni could pass by such tempting new lands without bothering to go ashore. Leif decided to do more than just talk. To his mind, these new lands were begging to be explored. And who better to explore them than he? Tall, strapping, and good-looking, Leif was thoughtful as well as adventurous, and shrewd as well as honest. True, he was barely over twenty-one years old, but he had been sailing since he was a boy. For a teacher, he

Erik the Red's first shipload of settlers reaches Greenland in A.D. 983.

had had his own father, Erik the Red. And Erik had been the original settler in Greenland many years earlier. Leif came by his love of adventure naturally!

Leif set about making his preparations. First, he visited Bjarni Herjolfsson. He quizzed the merchant closely about sailing directions to the new lands he had sighted southwest of Greenland. Then he bought Bjarni's ship. If it had sailed safely across the Western Ocean once, it could do so again!

Next Leif put together a crew. Thirty-five of Greenland's best seamen were soon signed up for the voyage. In a shrewd move, Leif asked his father to lead the expedition. Greenland colonists clearly looked to Erik the Red as their leader. His courage and daring seamanship had established the Greenland colony. Who better to lead this new expedition?

Bronze sculpture showing the plan of Brattahlid, Erik the Red's farm, at the ruins site in Greenland

At first Erik refused Leif's invitation. He was getting too old for such a voyage, he explained regretfully. He just wasn't up to the rigors of hard times at sea. But Leif wouldn't take no for an answer. His father was still the best man for the job, he argued. Of all the Greenlanders, Erik could surely command a successful voyage. Finally, Erik gave way to his persuasive son. If it meant so much to Leif, Erik would lead the expedition. Relieved, Leif had his ship outfitted and a sailing date set. The voyage was on!

One fine summer's morning, Leif and Erik set out on horseback to the ship's docking. When they were almost at the water, Erik's horse stumbled. Erik was thrown off, spraining his ankle. The old Norseman took this as a sign. "It is not my destiny to discover

Leif Eriksson and his crew approaching an unknown coast

any more lands," he told his son. "Here we must part ways." And so saying, he turned his horse and returned home.

If Leif was disappointed by this turn of events, he didn't let it show. What the father wouldn't do, the son could. Leif went directly to where his ship rode at anchor. Without delay, he and his men hoisted sail and headed off into the unknown western sea.

Now all that was in the past. Leif and his men had long since left Greenland's shores behind them. Steering by the sun by day and the stars by night, they should soon be coming to Bjarni's lands.

Sure enough, off to the west, Leif spotted an island. Excitedly, he hailed his crewmates. They sailed closer, cast anchor, and went ashore on the ship's rowboat.

This new land wasn't very impressive. There was no grass, just a long slab of flat rock stretching from the sea to a background of great icy glaciers. Like Bjarni before him, Leif was hard-pressed to find anything good to say about such a barren place. "At least we made it ashore," he finally commented, remembering how Bjarni had sailed by without even stopping. "I shall call this land Helluland, Flatstone Land."

Leif and his men returned to their ship and continued sailing south and west. The next land they spotted was flat and wooded, with long, sandy beaches running from the sea to the forest. Again the men cast anchor and went ashore on the small boat. "This land too shall be named according to its nature," announced Leif. "It shall be called Markland—Wood Land."

The men didn't spend much time exploring before they returned to their ship. Bidding Markland farewell, they put out to sea with a northeast wind. Two days went by, and they caught sight of land again. This time, things looked more promising. There was a small island lying just offshore of the mainland, and they decided to land there first.

It was a beautiful day—clear skies, sparkling blue water, and a glittering of dew still on the grass. Leif and his men ran their fingers over the dew and tasted it. They all agreed that they had never tasted anything so sweet.

Anxious to set foot on the mainland, the Norsemen hurried back to their ship. They sailed into a channel between the island and the cape of the mainland, heading west around the cape. Here the tide was at low ebb, and the ship ran aground in the shallow water. Not bothering to wait for high tide, the men rowed to shore in their small boat.

Once on shore, Leif and his men found a river leading from the channel into an inland lake. As soon as the tide was high enough, they rowed back to the ship and brought it up the river to anchor in the lake. Carrying their sheepskin sleeping bags and other supplies off the ship, they set up temporary huts so that they could live comfortably ashore.

It didn't take Leif and his men long to realize what a choice spot they had happened upon. Salmon—larger than any they had ever seen before—were abundant in both the river and the lake. A spruce forest to the south would provide wood for building and fuel. Lush meadowland would feed any livestock that might follow on future voyages. With all these natural advantages, the Norsemen decided to replace their temporary shelters with the larger houses of a permanent camp.

Spring salmon in St. Mary's River, Nova Scotia

Shelters built at the Vinland settlement

As the winter wore on, Leif and his men discovered more marvels. No frost came to wither the grass—an unheard-of condition for these Norsemen. Then, too, the winter days and nights more equal in length than in Greenland or Iceland. Why, even on the shortest day of winter the sun was up from breakfast time until well into the afternoon!

Once they had finished building their houses, Leif sent his men out to explore their new home. His rules were strict. Half the men would stay at the camp each day, while half explored the countryside. At no time was anyone to wander so far that he couldn't return by nightfall. And under no circumstances were the men to get separated from each other.

In spite of Leif's orders, one of the men—a German named Tyrkir—didn't return to camp one evening. Leif was more than usually upset. Tyrkir was a longtime family friend and had been like a second father to Leif throughout his childhood. Giving his shipmates the rough edge of his tongue for losing Tyrkir, Leif quickly organized a search party.

They hadn't gone far when they met Tyrkir coming back to meet them. The German clearly had news, but for a while he was so excited that he spoke only in his native tongue, which none of the rest could understand. Finally Leif calmed him down enough that he could speak in Norse. "I have something wonderful to report! Though I only went a little way further than you, I have found vines and grapes!"

Artist's vision of the Vikings' discovery of grapes in Vinland

Today, no grapes grow in the region believed to be Vinland, but they may have at the time of the Viking discovery.

"Is this true?" demanded Leif. If so, it really *was* wonderful news. Grapes didn't grow in Greenland, and wine made from grapes was a real luxury. Leif was already planning to bring back a load of timber to sell to the Greenlanders. If he could add a cargo of grapes as well, his profit was assured.

"Of course it's true!" said Tyrkir, indignant that his crewmates thought he couldn't recognize grapes when he saw them. "I was born where there are plenty of vines and grapes!"

Now Leif and his men were doubly busy. Besides exploring the countryside and keeping their ship in good repair, they set to work felling timber and gathering grapes for their return cargo. By winter's end, the hold was fully loaded.

When spring came, Leif and his crewmates readied their ship and sailed for home. As they pulled away from shore, Leif performed one last duty. As he had in the other two places they had explored, he named this new land, calling it Vinland, or Wineland. For all the good things the crew had found there, it was often called Vinland the Good.

The return trip to Greenland was uneventful, except for one incident. Just off the home coast, Leif spotted fifteen shipwrecked men and women. Always big-hearted, Leif rescued them from the reef upon which they had foundered. For this, and for his discovery of Vinland the Good, he was thereafter known as Leif the Lucky.

In later years, Vinland the Good would be recognized as America the beautiful. Scholars now agree that Leif's Helluland is most likely Baffin Island, which lies some 300 miles (483 kilometers) west of Greenland in the Canadian Arctic. Markland sounds very much like Labrador, another 600 miles (966 kilometers) to the south. And Vinland itself? Vinland has been placed everywhere from Canada to Maryland. Most scholars today agree that Vinland is really the northern tip of the island of Newfoundland.

And so, nearly five hundred years before Christopher Columbus set sail, Leif the Lucky, that intrepid Norseman from Greenland, became the first European to set foot in North America.

Gull Island Falls, Conception Bay, Newfoundland

Chapter 2
The Fury of the Norsemen

By all accounts, Leif Eriksson was fair-minded and honest as well as adventurous—a genuine leader of men. But Leif was also descended from a long line of Vikings and was a junior member of a most quarrelsome family. In fact, were Leif *not* from such a quarrelsome Viking family, he might never have made his famous voyage to Vinland in the first place. His journey, extraordinary as it was, was just the latest in a series of similar voyages that took place throughout the Viking Age.

The Vikings, or Norsemen, flourished from around the middle of the eighth century A.D. to the end of the eleventh century. They lived in Scandinavia (Norway, Sweden, and Denmark), and some later moved to Iceland and Greenland. For 250 years, Vikings were adventurers and pirates, and the Viking Age is remembered most for its raiding and plundering.

Viking explorers landing on unknown shores

Much of what is known about the Vikings today was recorded by the victims of their raids. Naturally, these people did not speak very highly of their attackers. Through the years, Vikings have come to have a reputation for cruelty and ruthlessness. Certainly their code of honor seemed to demand crude manliness over manners or virtue. By today's standards, Viking "justice" seems a lot like revenge. But the Vikings weren't all bad. Like people everywhere, they had their strengths and their weaknesses.

Much about the Viking Age is still a mystery today. Scholars cannot even agree on exactly where the Vikings got their name. The word "Viking" may have come from the Old Norse word *vikingr*, which meant "sea-raider" or "pirate." It may have come from another Old Norse word, *vik*, which meant "bay"—referring to the sheltering bays where the Norsemen

Norse farmers trying to raise crops on their rocky land

lurked in their swift-sailing pirate ships. Or it may have been adapted from an actual place name, the Vik, a coastal area near Oslo, Norway.

But scholars do know some things about the Vikings. First, their native world was rather limited. Though Scandinavia covers a large geographical area, very little of the land in Norway, Sweden, and Denmark can support human life. About one-third of Scandinavian land lies within the Arctic Circle. Even more land consists of rocky, barren tundra, or cold, inhospitable mountains. Pockets of fertile farmland have always been scarce.

Whatever farmland Viking families had, they guarded well. On farms tucked between dense forests and forbidding mountains, isolated during long, severe, northern winters, Norsemen learned to be self-reliant and fiercely independent.

They also learned to be excellent sailors and boat builders. Seamanship was a necessity for the people of Scandinavia. They were enclosed by thousands of miles of coastline inset with bays and inlets and fjords, or narrow sea channels between steep cliffs. Surrounding waters were dotted with still more thousands of islands. Rough terrain made road-building so difficult that, if a Viking family didn't have a boat, they didn't go anywhere.

By the middle of the eighth century, their native lands had proven too small for them, and the Vikings were going everywhere. The Swedes moved across the Baltic Sea into Russia. (The name "Russia" comes from the Swedish word *Rus*, the name for Swedes in those days.) They traveled down the great Russian rivers to the Black and Caspian seas, all the way to

The funeral of Rurik, a Viking who, in 862, set up a ruling dynasty in what is now Russia

the mighty Byzantine Empire in the Mediterranean area. Along the way they traded (or raided) for silver, furs, precious stones, spices, silks, wine, ivory, fruit, honey—and human slaves. For, fiercely as they protected their own personal freedom, the Norsemen had no qualms about depriving others of their liberty. In fact, their whole way of life depended on slaves, or thralls, as they were then called. Someone had to work the farms while the owners were off raiding and plundering!

The Danes, on the other hand, headed south and southwest. England and France bore the brunt of their attacks. An entire province in France was renamed "Normandy" after these conquerors from the north. Eventually, Danish Vikings also fell upon Spain, Italy, Sicily, Portugal, and even Morocco in northern Africa.

The Norseman Rolf attacking what is now Paris, France

The Norwegians were busy in Europe, too. Sometimes they joined forces with the Danes in their exploits. But they turned their sights westward as well. England, Scotland, Ireland; the Shetland, Orkney, and Faeroe islands—all were fair game for Norwegian Vikings. In fact, the earliest recorded Viking raids were almost all carried out by Norwegians.

Imagine the scene. Out of the north, a barely visible speck appears on the horizon. As it nears, it shows itself to be a ship, long and low-slung, with a single square sail. Closer still, and as many as sixty leather-helmeted, blond-bearded warriors are seen manning the oars. Rising from the prow is a fierce dragon's head, painted blood-red and inlaid with gold. With horrifying speed, the warriors beach their ship and pour over its low sides. Yelling a blood-curdling battle cry, this human river spreads over the land. Broadswords flashing, the Vikings plunder everything in their path. Jewels, weapons, livestock, gold, human hostages—nothing and nobody is safe. Anyone foolish enough to resist is cruelly struck down.

Then, almost before the raid is truly begun, it ends. The blond marauders race back to their ship, push off, and disappear again into the northern horizon. Time and again, just such a scene was played out throughout Europe, giving rise to the fervent prayer, "Deliver us, O Lord, from the fury of the Northmen!"

Griffon head ornament from a Viking helmet

Viking raids such as these were usually carried out by men intent on personal gain—a younger son, perhaps, whose family lands in Scandinavia were no longer large enough to support both him and his older brother. But these raids are only part of the story. Often, the Norsemen were on legitimate trading voyages. Instead of stealing, they bartered and bought

An artist's rendition of Norse settlers arriving in a faraway land

the goods they wanted. Sometimes the Vikings were on organized political or military expeditions. Then their aim was to subdue a native population and establish in its place a ruling Norse empire.

Whatever their reasons, for over two hundred years the Vikings overran their national boundaries to penetrate faraway lands. Gradually, the Viking overflow turned into flourishing colonies in the host countries. The people from the north married and raised families in their new lands. Their children, and their children's children, became legitimate citizens—natives—of countries as diverse as Russia, France, Great Britain, and Ireland. Today, millions of families around the world can trace their ancestry back to these Viking adventurers from the north.

Chapter 3
"It Was Now That Iceland Was Discovered"

Leif Eriksson was one such person who could trace his ancestry back to Viking Norway. His story begins with his grandfather, and before that, with the Viking discovery and settlement of Iceland.

By the middle of the ninth century, the Viking expansion had spread to the islands of the North Atlantic Ocean. The Shetlands, the Orkneys, the Hebrides, the Faeroes—like a series of stepping stones, these island colonies extended Norse rule farther and farther west. Now the Vikings were about to take a gigantic new step westward.

It all began around A.D. 860, with a Swede named Gardar. Gardar was married to a Norwegian woman, whose father had just willed her some land in the Hebrides. Gardar lost no time sailing for the Hebrides, some 500 miles (805 kilometers) to the west, to claim his wife's inheritance.

On the way, a fierce gale drove Gardar off course and took him far out into the North Atlantic Ocean. Curious about a new land that he saw ahead, Gardar decided to do a little investigating. Past icy mountains and rushing rivers, beyond a long, flat harborless coastline, Gardar sailed on in a southwesterly course. When the coastline turned north, he came into a huge bay rimmed with mountains and volcanoes. Farther north was another huge bay, dotted with islands, reefs, and treacherous currents.

The intrepid Gardar sailed on. Soon he passed icefalls, or frozen waterfalls, tumbling straight into the sea, and huge, rocky cliffs. Rounding the northern cape of this new land, he headed southeast along a flatter, greener, gentler coastline. He pushed on. Summer was ending, and he knew that the harsh northern winter would soon prevent him from sailing any farther.

Finally Gardar anchored his ship in a natural harbor backed by a steep, rocky cliff. He quickly built a sheltering house, named the place Husavik, or House Bay, and spent a comfortable winter no more than 40 miles (64 kilometers) south of the Arctic Circle.

When spring came, Gardar hoisted sail and continued his voyage. Now the coastline jutted to the northeast, forcing Gardar to guide his ship well into the Arctic Circle. One last jutting peninsula, and Gardar headed south again. The landscape began to look familiar, and Gardar realized that he had sailed around an entire island. Well pleased with himself, Gardar sailed some 700 miles (1,127 kilometers) home to Scandinavia. He spoke highly of this new land and, not being an overly modest man, he named the island Gardarsholm.

Vatnajokull, one of Iceland's inland glaciers and the largest glacier in Europe. Glaciers like this one are built up as more snow falls than melts.

Not long after Gardar's journey, another Viking happened onto these same shores. By all accounts, Naddod the Viking was a great man but had his fair share of enemies. Naddod was on his way to make a home for himself in the Faeroes, "for the good reason that he had nowhere else he would be safe." Like Gardar, he, too, was blown off course to the island in the Western Ocean.

Naddod wasn't the intrepid sailor that Gardar was. Rather than follow the coastline, he beached his ship and climbed a mountain to check for signs of human habitation. Not finding any, he returned to his ship and sailed back home. As he pulled out of harbor, a heavy snowstorm blew up. Because of this, Naddod named the island Snaeland, or Snowland.

To help him find Iceland, Floki brought ravens on his voyage. The one that flew away and never came back had found land. This gave Floki the nickname Raven-Floki.

Naddod praised Snaeland highly when he returned to Scandinavia. A third Viking, Floki Vilgerdarson, liked what he heard. For the first time in Viking history, a Norseman set out intentionally to find this new land in the west. But Floki didn't plan just to explore the new land. Loading his ship with livestock and other homesteading supplies, Floki intended to settle permanently in Snaeland.

At first all went well. Following Naddod's sailing directions, Floki reached Snaeland safely and built a hall on the far side of the great bay called Breidafjord. It was a glorious summer. There was fine pasturage for the livestock, a fjord full of fish and seals, and a long succession of balmy summer days.

Too late, Floki and his crewmates realized that summer wouldn't last forever. Winter came, and the green pastures were covered with snow and ice. No one had thought to make hay while the sun shone, and the fine Norwegian cattle all starved to death.

Spring finally came, but it was cold and wet. Climbing a mountain to survey the countryside, the disgruntled Floki saw only a long fjord, choked with drifting ice. Taking this as his inspiration, Floki gave the island yet a third name, and the one by which we know it today—Iceland.

Things went from bad to worse. Giving up thoughts of a permanent settlement, Floki and his crew tried to head home to Norway. Unexpected gales blew their ship back to shore, and the Norsemen were forced to spend a second winter on this icy, inhospitable island. When they finally made their way back to Norway, Floki had nothing but bad things to say about Iceland. A crewmate named Herjolf had both good and bad to say of it, and another crewmate, Thorolf, "swore that butter dripped from every blade of grass." For his extravagant praise, Thorolf was ever after known as Thorolf Butter.

At least two Vikings were so impressed by Thorolf's description that they wanted to settle in Iceland permanently. Ingolf and Leif were cousins and foster-brothers, and they were true Vikings. One summer they went on a raiding cruise with three brothers named Holmstein, Herstein, and Hastein. The raid went well, and plans were made to go again the following summer. Ingolf and Leif threw a party for Holmstein, Herstein, and Hastein in celebration of their friendship and good fortune.

Unfortunately, the party didn't turn out well. In the middle of the festivities, Holmstein announced his intentions to marry Ingolf's sister, Helga. The only problem was that Leif was also in love with Helga. As the story is told, when he heard Holmstein's announcement, Leif "turned red, and there was little love lost between him and Holmstein when they parted at feast's end."

Ingolf and Leif apparently forgot about the quarrel over the winter. Next spring they set out as planned to meet their friends for another raid. But when they arrived at the agreed-upon meeting place, Holmstein and his brothers attacked them. In the fight that followed, Holmstein was killed and his brothers fled. Ingolf and Leif simply went on with their raid.

When the cousins returned to Norway, they got wind of Herstein's plan to avenge his brother's death in true Viking fashion. Not waiting for Herstein to move, Ingolf and Leif decided to attack first. Once again there was a fierce fight, and this time Herstein was killed.

Now the cousins were getting worried. They were true Vikings, and they probably felt justified in killing Holmstein and Herstein. But the dead men were sons of a nobleman, and Hastein was still alive to seek vengeance for his brothers' deaths. Ingolf and Leif knew they'd have to pay for the killings eventually.

Being practical fellows, they decided to pay in cash rather than with their lives. Sending friends to sue for peace, the cousins soon struck a deal. They would give Hastein and his noble father all their lands and worldly goods. In exchange, the cousins could keep their lives.

That's when Leif and Ingolf started thinking about Floki's Iceland. They'd lost all their holdings in Norway and couldn't be sure that Hastein wasn't still bearing a grudge. The island refuge of Iceland offered land and safety—two things the Viking cousins needed most.

So they set off on an initial voyage of exploration. They found Iceland without any difficulty and spent the winter scouting the countryside for good homesteading sites. Then they returned to Norway to put their affairs in order for a permanent move. While Ingolf laid out what little money they had left for supplies, Leif went raiding in Ireland.

As the medieval Icelandic history book *Landnamabok (The Book of the Settlements)* tells the story, "Leif went raiding in Ireland, where he found a large house, which he entered. All was dark, until a light shone from a sword that a man was holding. Leif killed this man, and took the sword from him and great riches, too. From then on he was known as Hjorleif, Sword-Leif. Hjorleif raided far and wide in Ireland, winning great riches there, and taking captive ten thralls."

With his booty in hand, Hjorleif returned to Norway, where he and Ingolf hurriedly outfitted their boats and set sail. Alas, Hjorleif's ten Irish thralls were to prove his undoing. When the cousins reached Iceland, they separated and settled in different regions. Hjorleif put his thralls to work clearing the land, while he built two fine halls.

The Irishmen, however, were still furious about being kidnapped, and they certainly didn't like pulling plows like common oxen. So they plotted to kill Hjorleif and his men. Once they'd succeeded in their bloodthirsty plot, the Irishmen gathered up all of Hjorleif's riches, took the Norse women captive, and set sail for a group of islands they spotted in the southwest.

Waterfall in the Romsdalen Valley of western Norway. The rocky land in Norway, where many Vikings originated, made poor farmland. This drove many to make settlements elsewhere.

Norse ship

They didn't have long to enjoy their freedom. Ingolf soon learned of his cousin's untimely death. The *Landnamabok* gives this account of the events that followed:

"When he saw Hjorleif lying dead, he was deeply moved. This is what he said, 'This is a sorry end for a brave man.' Ingolf had Hjorleif and his men buried and took charge of their ship and their share of the property. Ingolf then walked up to the cliff and could see islands lying to the southwest. It struck him that the thralls would have run off there, because the boat had disappeared. So away he went to look for them.

"The thralls were eating a meal when Ingolf surprised them. Panic overwhelmed them, and they ran each his own way. Ingolf killed them all. Many of them jumped off the cliff which has since been known

An Icelander's home, built of stone and sod

by their name. The islands where these thralls were killed have been known ever since as the Vestmannaeyjar, because they were Vestmenn, Irishmen."

Ingolf took the captured Norse women back to Iceland and proceeded to establish the first permanent colony on that island. As the *Landnamabok* says, "Ingolf was the most famous of all settlers, for he came to an unlived-in country and was the first to settle down in it. The other settlers did so by his example."

The *Landnamabok* goes on to tell the stories of some four hundred of Iceland's original settlers, who came with their families, slaves, livestock, and supplies to carve new lives for themselves on Iceland's shores. In just sixty years, essentially all of Iceland's habitable land had been taken.

Who were these settlers, and why did they leave their homes in Norway to become pioneers in an unknown land? To begin, some of them really didn't have much in the way of homes to leave. Norway, with its limited land resources, was having trouble supporting an ever-growing population. Like pioneers throughout history, the Icelandic Vikings were drawn by the prospect of vast unclaimed lands to the west.

But it was more than a desire for new lands that brought the Norsemen to Iceland. There was also Harald Haarfagr—King Harald Fairhair of Norway.

In the early part of the Viking Age, Norway was a cluster of small, independent states composed mainly of members of the same family or clan. There was no central government and not even an attempt at a

Castle built by Norse explorers on a conquered coast

central government, until a man named Halfdan the Black took over a group of mini-states near present-day Oslo in 841. Halfdan called himself a monarch. Still, it wasn't until his son, Harald Fairhair, conquered the rest of Norway some forty years later that Norway really became unified under one king.

Not all Norwegians were happy to belong to a unified country. Vikings were notoriously independent, and many resented King Harald's attempts to control them. They resented the taxes he imposed—pure robbery!—and the loss of lands he seized as he carved out his kingdom. And, naturally, the chieftains Harald had battled to become king resented their defeat at his hands.

To Norwegians who remained in Norway and enjoyed the peace and stability of national unity, Harald appeared wise and capable. To those who fled his power, he was nothing less than a villain. The historical tale known as *Egils Saga* describes the situation:

"Once he had taken possession of his new territories, King Harald paid close attention to the noblemen and leading farmers, and all those from whom he suspected some rebellion might be looked for. He made everyone either become his subjects or leave the country, or, for a third choice, suffer hardship or forfeit their lives; while some were maimed hand or foot. King Harald seized possession of the entire land, settled and unsettled, and the sea and the waters, too, and all the men must become his tenants, and those too who worked in the forests, and all the hunters and fishers by sea and land—all these were now made subject to him. But many a man fled the land from this servitude. . . . And it was now that Iceland was discovered."

An island in the Orkneys

Some of the disgruntled Vikings came directly to Iceland from Norway. Others fled Norway for the already settled western islands—Ireland and Britain, the Shetlands, Orkneys, Hebrides, and Faeroes. But Harald didn't like having rebellious Viking chiefs so near his own shores. He sent his royal fleet to find and destroy the exiled warriors. Many of those who managed to escape Harald's sword did so by fleeing to Iceland.

Even the determined Harald realized that Iceland was too far away for him to constantly chase after rebellious chiefs. So he let them go. For a while Harald tried to claim sovereignty of Iceland, but the Icelanders didn't pay much attention. As far as they were concerned, Harald might rule Norway, but he would

Thingvellir, site of the first Althing meetings in Iceland

never rule them. They set up their own general assembly, the *Althing*, elected a "lawspeaker" or president, made a constitution, and became a republic.

Still, economic and family ties remained strong between Iceland and Norway. Iceland's settlers depended on Norway for the supplies they needed to build their new colonies. Iceland might be rich in pasturage and fine fishing. But it didn't have timber for building houses, metal for making tools, or even much arable land for growing grain to feed hungry children. Norway, in turn, was interested in the exports Iceland could supply. Icelanders raised sheep for wool and sheepskins, they raised cows for butter and cheese, and they captured and trained the wild falcons so prized for the sport of falconry in all of Europe.

Then, too, almost all of the Icelandic colonists still had family and friends back in Norway. No one wanted to cut off ties completely.

Iceland and Norway finally arrived at a truce. It was agreed that Norway would have some influence, if not actual authority, in Icelandic affairs. In return, Icelanders were allowed to keep their Norwegian citizenship. It was an uneasy truce, but a truce all the same. And it managed to last for over three hundred years.

The Vikings (Swedes and Danes, as well as Norwegians) made Iceland a thriving country. But they weren't the island's first inhabitants. By the end of the eighth century A.D., before the Vikings had arrived, Irish monks, or *papar*, were living along much of the southeast coast. Sailing 800 miles (1,416 kilometers) north and west from Ireland in small skin-covered boats called *curraghs*, they came to Iceland to escape the corruptions of the civilized world. In tiny cells hidden high on rocky cliffs, these gentle Irish monks gloried in their isolation and offered up lives of devotion to God.

It must have been a shock to these religious hermits when the first square-sailed Viking ship sailed into Icelandic waters. As Irishmen, they were well aware of the Viking temperament. With sinking hearts, they could easily foretell the end of their quiet lives of prayer and worship.

Then, too, the monks knew that the Norsemen were not Christian. Since living among heathens was contrary to all they believed in, the Irish monks left Iceland as quietly as they had come. As the medieval *Book of the Icelanders*, the *Islendingabok*, tells it: "There were Christian men here then whom the

A medieval monk

Norsemen call 'papar.' But they went away because they were not prepared to live in the company of heathen men. They left behind Irish books, bells, and crosiers [staffs], from which it could be seen that they were Irishmen."

After the papar "went away," Iceland was left to the Norsemen. Except for that one brief Irish footnote, Iceland's history belongs to Ingolf the Viking and his fellow settlers from the north.

Chapter 4
A Quarrelsome Family, Another New Land

Ingolf built his house at Reykjavik, or Smoky Bay, around A.D. 875. By A.D. 930, all of Iceland's best land was settled. Some five-sixths of the country was uninhabitable sandy beaches, lava fields, rocky mountains, and icy glacial fields. But along the fjords and at the base of the mountains, long valleys offered lush pastures that invited settlement. In was in these grassy nooks and hollows that the early colonists made their homes.

Leif Eriksson's grandfather was not one of the original Icelandic settlers. In fact, by the time grandfather Thorvald, son of Asvald, reached Iceland around A.D. 960, all the good land had been taken. (Thorvald did have some claim to Iceland, however. *His* grandfather, Ulf Oxen-Thorir, was brother to the Viking Naddod, who had discovered Iceland as Snaeland some hundred years earlier.)

Thorvald didn't come to Iceland to escape the wrath of King Harald, who was long-since dead. He didn't come because of the lure of new land, since all the best land in Iceland had already been taken. As the historical tale titled *Erik the Red's Saga* tells it, "There was a man by the name of Thorvald who was the son of Asvald, son of Ulf Oxen-Thorir's son. Thorvald's son was called Erik the Red, and both father and son left Jaeder [in Norway] because of some killings."

Like so many Vikings before and after him, Thorvald was a hot-tempered man. No further details are given about these killings. But whatever the circumstances, they were bad enough that Thorvald took his wife, daughter, and red-headed son Erik on a 1,000-mile (1,609-kilometer) sea voyage to Iceland.

Since the best land had already been claimed, Thorvald and his family contented themselves with a rocky farm on Iceland's barren northwest coast. They lived here uneventfully until Thorvald's death.

Some time after his father died, Erik married a girl from southern Iceland named Thjodhild. He and his wife then left the barren north country to clear a new and greener farm in her home territory of Haukadal. They weren't to enjoy this new farm for long. It seems that Erik had inherited his father's hot temper, and he was soon involved in a bloody family feud.

It began when two of Erik's thralls started a landslide that crashed down on and destroyed a neighbor's farm. Since the Viking code of honor called for people to seek their own justice, the neighbor and his friends promptly killed Erik's thralls. Not one to stand by for such an insult, Erik killed the men who had killed his thralls. But now he was in trouble.

Erik the Red

According to Icelandic law, thralls were property, not people. Killing them was bad, since it destroyed another man's property, but killing a free man was murder. So Erik the Red, a newcomer to Haukadal, was charged with killing two prominent, long-time citizens. *Erik the Red's Saga* states his punishment clearly: "Erik was thrown out of Haukadal."

Erik took his family to the island of Oxney in the bay of Breidafjord. But even here, Erik couldn't stay out of trouble. In a quarrel with a friend over the legal ownership of some household goods, Erik managed to kill two of his friend's sons.

Now Erik had two powerful families out for his blood. At the Althing, the Icelandic assembly of law, Erik was banished from Iceland for three years. Until he left, he was fair game for his enemies.

Erik wasn't without friends and supporters. These friends hid Erik and helped him outfit a ship while his enemies combed the land for him. When the ship was ready, Erik's friends escorted him past the islands west of Iceland. Promising to return the favor whenever it was in his power to do so, Erik set his sights westward and bid his friends farewell.

Where exactly did Erik think he was going as he sailed into the Western Sea? He could more easily have headed east, back to his childhood home in Norway. Or he could have set out on a raiding expedition to the British Isles. Either would have been perfectly honorable for a Viking to do. But Erik was made of more adventurous stuff. Instead of looking backwards, he looked forward. For two hundred years, the Vikings had been extending the western boundary of the known world. Now Erik planned to push that boundary a little bit farther. He was going to find Gunnbjorn's Skerries!

No one today knows exactly where Gunnbjorn's Skerries really were. We know only that they were a group of small, rocky islands that lay a two- to four-day sail west of Iceland. They had been discovered by accident sometime between A.D. 900 and 930, when a man named Gunnbjorn Ulf-Krakuson was blown off course as he sailed the western coast of Iceland. Like Gardar, Naddod, and other storm-tossed Vikings before him, Gunnbjorn brought home exciting tales of new lands to the west.

Gunnbjorn's family lived in the same corner of Iceland where Erik had spent his youth. No doubt Erik had heard the tales of Gunnbjorn's Skerries—and of the larger land that lay still farther to the west—as he was growing up. Now, exiled from Ice-

Snaefellsjokul, an ice-covered peak in Iceland

land and possessed of an adventurous nature, it was only natural that he should try to find these lands for himself.

So Erik and his crew set out. They didn't have a compass to establish directions and keep them on a straight course, but they did have the Icelandic peak named Snaefellsjokul (Snowfell Glacier). Rising some 4,700 feet (1,433 meters) high, Snaefellsjokul could be seen at sea for over 90 miles (145 kilometers). As long as Erik kept Snaefellsjokul in view, he could steer a straight course. When the icy peak had passed out of sight, he still had the sun and the stars by which to steer the westerly course Gunnbjorn had described.

Erik did have at least one mechanical device to help him navigate. For years Norse seamen had used what is called "latitude sailing." They couldn't find their longitude—their position in terms of east and west. However, they *could* locate their latitude, or position in terms of north and south. One way was by using an instrument known as a bearing-dial, similar to the astrolabe used by ancient Greek sailors. The bearing-dial was a notched wooden disk with a rotating smooth edge. Sailors used it to mark the azimuth, or position of a star in its regular arc across the sky. By carefully noting the azimuth of the sun or the North Star, sailors could keep a true east-west course.

Norse sailors also used a device called a sun-shadow board. This was a wooden disk marked with concentric circles. A vertical stick set in the middle of this disk was raised or lowered, depending on the season and the sun's position in the sky. (The Norse had guides known as "declination tables" that told how high to set the stick each week.) At high noon, the sun-shadow board was floated in a tub of water to make it level. Sailors could then "read" the position of the stick's shadow in relation to the circles on the disk to tell their ship's latitude.

Still, these instruments were crude at best, and neither worked when the sun and stars were hidden from view. Some people think Norse sailors used yet another device, one that revealed the sun's position even when it was covered with clouds. The sagas mention certain magic "sun stones," which scholars believe could have been light-sensitive crystals of calcite or spar. Both these minerals are found in Scandinavia, and both can, indeed, be used to locate the sun even when it is hidden by clouds or fog.

Navigational instruments used by various seamen in history

Finally, the Norsemen, like sailors everywhere, relied on their enormous body of sea lore. The color of the water, the size and strength of currents and wave swells, the presence or absence of seaweed and driftwood, the migratory patterns of marine creatures and sea birds, the "feel" of a wind—all worked to help the sharp-witted seamen navigate a safe course.

Whatever their navigational tools, Erik and his crewmates set off on their westward way. In a few days, their labors were rewarded—sort of. There was, indeed, land ahead. But what an icy, inhospitable land it appeared! A huge icecap rose from its center, and menacing glaciers dotted its rocky coast.

Erik turned his ship southward, hoping to find more hospitable shores. He sailed westward around a rocky cape and headed back up the northwestern coast. This was more like it! Thousands of seabirds swooped and called from a sea dotted with islands. On the shore, deep fjords led to green, grassy meadows and countless natural harbors.

For three summers Erik explored the western coast of this new land. Islands, fjords, headlands, and meadows—Erik scouted them all for habitable land. And whatever he saw, he named. In the winters, he and his crew rested from their explorations. They anchored their ship, built shelters of sod, fished, and hunted the bear, reindeer, seal, and walrus so abundant in this new land.

Eriksfjord, on the southwestern coast of Greenland, where Erik the Red built a settlement

By the time Erik's three years of exile were over, he had scouted some 1,000 miles (1,609 kilometers) of coastline. Convinced that this new land was ripe for colonizing, he sailed the 750 miles (1,207 kilometers) back to Iceland. As the sagas say, "The following summer Erik returned to Iceland. . . . He called the country he had discovered Greenland, for he argued that men would be drawn to go there if the land had an attractive name." In his determination to attract settlers to his new land, Erik the explorer had become Erik the land promoter.

Walruses provided the Greenland settlers with leather, meat, and fat

Back home in Iceland, Erik managed to get into one last fight with the man whose sons he had killed. Erik lost the fight and, tired of the feuding and anxious to get on with his Greenland venture, he managed to patch up the feud once and for all. Then he was finally free to organize his expedition to Greenland.

It turned out to be quite an expedition. Life in Iceland had never been easy. There were many land-hungry, adventure-loving souls eager to try their luck in Erik's Greenland. Then, too, some ten years earlier, around 976, a great famine had swept over Iceland. Scores of people had died. Discouraged by this setback, many of the survivors must have reasoned that things could hardly be worse in a new land. And according to Erik the Red, this particular new land was teeming with wildlife, fine pastureland, and friendly harbors.

In the summer of 986, Erik sailed out of Icelandic waters leading a fleet of some twenty-five ships. These were not the swift, low-slung fighting ships used in Viking raids. Instead of speed, Erik and his friends needed space, strength, and stability. Instead of a longship, they needed a *knarr*.

The Norse *knarr* was a large, broad-beamed merchant ship ideally suited to carry people, livestock, and cargo across wide stretches of water. Made of oak and pine secured by hundreds of iron rivets, the *knarr* had a deep keel, high sides, and a single mast and sail. The ship was designed so it could sail into the wind as well as before it. It also had a fixed steering board, or rudder, on the right side (hence the word "starboard" for the right side of a ship). Oar holes were cut into the ship's sides for rowing when there were calm winds, rough seas, or tricky anchorages. Sturdier than a fighting longship, the *knarr* could easily be handled by fifteen to twenty sailors.

In addition to the sailors, each *knarr* carried some ten to fifteen settlers and thralls, as well as the livestock and equipment they would need to start life in a new land. Half-decks in the front and back of the ship partially protected the people and cargo, and tents could be thrown up at night. Still, under breaking waves and falling rain and snow, no one stayed completely dry. No one was exempt from bailing the water out when leaks sprang up, either!

Since there was no way to cook on board, meals consisted mainly of cold breads, cheeses, and dried or smoked meats. Beer and mead took the place of fresh water for drinking. Nothing took the place of fresh water for washing, however, and crew and passengers alike were a pretty grimy bunch by the end of their voyage.

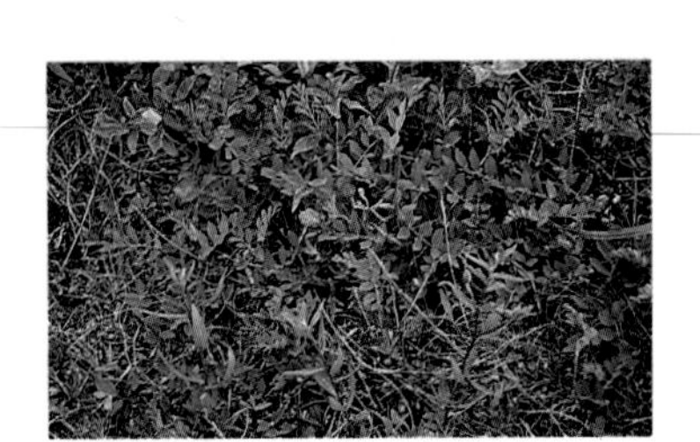

Wildflowers growing near Eriksfjord in Greenland

At least this time, Erik knew where he was going. Within four or five days, he had brought his fleet to Greenland's shores—or rather, part of his fleet. Of the twenty-five boats that set out, only fourteen reached Greenland. Of the other eleven boats, we know only

Ruins of a stable at Erik the Red's Brattahlid farm

what the sagas tell us: "Some were forced back, and some perished."

Still, some four hundred settlers *did* complete the journey safely. Following Erik's directions, they spread out along the island's fjord-ridden southwest coast. Most stayed in the southernmost area, which came to be known as the Eastern Settlement. Later, others traveled farther north, building homes in the smaller Western Settlement. For better or worse, the Icelandic colonizing of Greenland had begun. And another giant Norse step westward had been taken.

Chapter 5
Voyages to Vinland

Erik the Red was unquestionably Greenland's leading citizen. The farm he built at Brattahlid, at the northern head of Eriksfjord, was large and prosperous. It soon became the unofficial center of Greenland's social and political life. As the historic tale *The Greenlanders' Saga* says, "Erik the Red lived at Brattahlid; his state was one of high distinction, and all recognized his authority."

For some fourteen years, Erik and his family lived quietly at Brattahlid. Like the rest of the Greenland settlers, they were busy making homes for themselves in their adopted country.

There was plenty to do. Having no timber, they built houses and barns of stone, sod, and driftwood. Cattle and sheep were grazed in the summer; grass, hay, and meadow flowers had to be harvested for feed during the cold winter months. The thirteenth-century Norwegian guidebook known as *The King's Mirror* described colonial Greenland thus: "It is reported that the pasturage is good, and that there are large and fine farms in Greenland. . . . The earth yields good and fragrant grass. . . . The farmers raise cattle and sheep in large numbers, and make butter and cheese in great quantities. The people live chiefly on these foods and on beef, but they also eat the flesh of various kinds of game, such as reindeer, whales, seals, and bears."

Mother and pup harp seals (Pagophilus groenlandicus), *which inhabit North Atlantic and Arctic waters*

Turf hut built by hunters on an island off Greenland's coast

Some of the Greenland settlers were merchants as well as farmers and hunters. They filled their ships with Greenland's bounty—furs, hides, woolens, and dairy products, walrus ivory and seal oil, snow-white falcons and polar bears. Sailing to Iceland and then to Norway, they traded these goods for the items Greenlanders needed to survive. Timber, iron, tools and weapons, various grains, beer and wine, and European-style clothing—the exchange of these and other vital goods ensured regular contact between the European Norsemen and this remote outpost of Nordic life.

It was probably on just such a trading voyage that the young Leif Eriksson traveled when he visited King Olaf of Norway in the summer of A.D. 1000. Certainly Bjarni Herjolfsson was an established Norse merchant, with his own *knarr*, when he was blown off course into North American waters just a few months after Leif's father reached Greenland's shores in 986. As had happened so often in Norse history, the first sighting of a new land was made by a merchant. But it took an explorer of Leif Eriksson's vision and courage to follow up this accidental sighting with a deliberately planned voyage of exploration.

Leif Eriksson's historic journey to Vinland was only the first of several planned expeditions from Greenland to the North American continent. The very next one was made by his own brother, Thorvald.

When Leif returned from Vinland to the family seat at Brattahlid, Thorvald listened eagerly to his brother's stories. He liked what he heard, but he hadn't heard enough. In Thorvald's opinion, Leif had left much exploring undone. Thorvald proposed that he should lead another expedition to do things right.

Leif understood his younger brother's desire to see these new lands for himself. He agreed to let Thorvald use his ship for the journey, and even helped him outfit it with men and supplies. This time, there was no question of asking Erik the Red to lead the expedition. That grand old Viking had died during the previous winter. Leif was now head of the family.

And so, with Leif's blessing, Thorvald set out with his crew of thirty men. There is no record of their voyage until they reached Vinland, where they apparently went straight to Leif's permanent camp of Leifsbudir. (Scholars today believe that Leifsbudir was located on the western coast of Newfoundland.) They spent the winter there quietly, fishing for food and tending to any repairs their ship might need.

The following spring, Thorvald and his men set out exploring what was probably Newfoundland's western coast. According to *The Greenlanders' Saga,* "It looked to them a beautiful and well-wooded land, the woods hardly any distance from the sea, with white sands and a great many islands and shallows." The only sign of human life was a wooden grain bin.

Pleased with their explorations, they returned to Leifsbudir for a second winter. The next spring, Thorvald set out to explore the land to the north and east. This was probably Leif Eriksson's Markland, or today's Labrador. Though Thorvald found it lovely country, it was also to prove fatal for him.

Thorvald's ships sailing into a natural harbor

Unnamed pond in Newfoundland's Ferry Gulch

The trouble began when he and his crew met with heavy weather off a certain cape. They were driven ashore with a broken keel, which they had to spend a long time repairing. When the keel was finally seaworthy again, Thorvald named the cape Kjalarnes, or Keelness, in its honor.

Continuing their voyage, the Norsemen came to a wooded headland jutting out between two fjords. As they came ashore, Thorvald exclaimed over the beauty of the place and commented that this was a place where he'd like to live.

As they headed back to the ship, they spotted three mounds on the sandy beach. A closer examination revealed these to be three overturned canoes, each hiding three native men. True to their fighting nature, the Norsemen killed eight of the natives, the ninth escaping in his canoe.

The massacre was to have tragic consequences. As Thorvald and his men slept that night, they were attacked by "a countless fleet of canoes." Outnumbered, the Norsemen put up a protective fortification of boards on their ship and waited out the attack. Eventually, the natives, whom the Norse called Skraelings, grew tired and paddled away.

Ruins of a structure built by people of the Thule culture on Skraeling Island in the Arctic region of Canada. The island is named for early North Americans believed to be the ancestors of today's Eskimos.

Thorvald, wounded by an arrow

Quickly checking his men, Thorvald found that none had been injured. Then he admitted that he, however, had been struck by an arrow under his arm. Thorvald would die of the wound. Ever the commanding officer, he gave his last orders. His men were to bury him at the headland he had so admired and then make their preparations to sail back to Greenland.

The Greenlanders' Saga tells the rest of the story best: "Now Thorvald died. They . . . stayed there that winter gathering grapes and vines for the ship. The following spring they prepared to leave for Greenland, and brought their ship into Eriksfjord, and the news they had to tell Leif was big news indeed."

The big news of Thorvald's explorations and subsequent death spurred his younger brother Thorstein into action. Determined to bring home his brother's

Local legends say this spot on the cape of Massachusetts Bay is Thorvald's burial place.

body, Thorstein set out for Vinland in the same ship that Bjarni, Leif, and the unfortunate Thorvald had used. According to *The Greenlanders' Saga,* Thorstein took with him his wife, Gudrid (widow of one of the shipwrecked sailors Leif had rescued), possibly hoping to colonize Vinland with their future children.

But Thorstein's voyage proved unlucky, too. As *The Greenlanders' Saga* puts it, "They were storm-tossed the whole summer, had no notion where they were going, and after one week of winter finally reached land in Greenland, in the Western Settlement." Thorstein never had another chance to visit Vinland. That winter, he died from a sickness sweeping the Western Settlement. When summer came, Gudrid took his body home to Brattahlid, where it was laid to rest in the family church.

Now three of Erik the Red's children had voyaged, or tried to voyage, to Vinland the Good: Leif, Thorvald, and Thorstein. The story would not be complete, however, without an expedition by Erik's fourth child, his daughter Freydis. Freydis's voyage to Vinland was both fabulous and bloody, and many scholars today question whether it ever really happened. Still, the story of the voyage has come down through the ages in *The Greenlanders' Saga,* and as such it deserves to be heard.

Freydis's story starts with a pair of brothers from Iceland, Helgi and Finnbogi. Helgi and Finnbogi were on a trading voyage from Norway when they decided to spend the winter in Greenland. Freydis heard about the brothers (and about their seaworthy merchant ship) and decided to ask them to go with her on a voyage to Vinland.

Going to Vinland was by now considered both profitable and honorable, so Helgi and Finnbogi agreed to the voyage. Terms were soon struck. Freydis would take one ship, the brothers another. Each ship would be manned by thirty sailors, plus any women who wished to go along. Once in Vinland, they would all be free to use the houses Leif Eriksson had built at Leifsbudir.

Finally, Freydis and the brothers would share equally in whatever profit they brought back in the way of timber, grapes, furs, and other goods.

Freydis soon showed herself to be an untrustworthy woman. Instead of taking thirty seamen, Freydis took thirty-five, concealing the extra five until the ships reached Vinland. This, she reasoned, would give her the advantage in case any disagreements or fights broke out.

The ocean voyage was uneventful. Helgi and Finnbogi reached shore slightly ahead of Freydis, and the brothers began carrying their gear up to Leif's houses. But when Freydis landed, she challenged their right to do so. According to Freydis, Leif had loaned the houses to *her*, not to the party as a whole.

By now Helgi and Finnbogi were beginning to understand what kind of woman they were dealing with. Grumbling, they moved down the beach to build their own hall. While they were busy providing themselves and their crewmates with basic shelter, Freydis set her crew to work chopping down valuable timber for cargo.

When winter came, the brothers suggested various games and entertainments to pass the time. Things went well for a while, but then hostilities surfaced again. Soon, contact between the two houses was cut off entirely.

Perhaps it was the long, lonely winter that inspired her, or perhaps this had been Freydis's plan all along. In any case, one chilly night she crept out of the bed she shared with her husband, Thorvard of Gardar. Walking barefoot down the beach, she crept into the brothers' hall and woke Finnbogi. The two of them went outside to talk.

Freydis began the conversation innocently enough, asking Finnbogi how he liked Vinland. He replied that the country was fine, but that he was dismayed by the bitterness between the two camps. Freydis said that she felt the same way, and that that's why she had come to talk to him. The ill feelings had grown so strong, she wanted to leave Vinland. But first she wanted to trade ships with Finnbogi and Helgi, since they had the larger vessel.

Ruins of a medieval monastery at Igaliko, near Eriksfjord, Greenland. Once called Gardar, this area was the home Thorvard of Gardar, Freydis's husband.

Now, this clearly wasn't a fair trade. But Finnbogi must have been so relieved at the thought of being rid of Freydis that he readily agreed to the deal.

So they parted, each going back to bed. But even now, Freydis wasn't finished. Perhaps she had wanted Finnbogi to refuse her offer, so that she would have a reason to pick a quarrel. She lost no time in waking up Thorvard. Complaining that Finnbogi had refused her offer to buy (not trade for!) his boat, and that both brothers had beaten and abused her, Freydis demanded that Thorvard avenge her injury and shame.

The Greenlanders' Saga reports that Thorvard "could not endure this baiting of hers. He ordered his men to turn out and take up their weapons, and crossed straightway to the brothers' house and marched in on the sleeping men, seized them and bound them, then led them outside, each man as he was bound. And Freydis had each man killed as he came out."

That took care of the men. But there were still five women left in the Icelanders' hall. Even Freydis's hardened crew drew the line at killing women. When no one stepped forward to remove these witnesses to Freydis's bloody slaughter, she snatched up a battle-axe and did the deed herself.

Norse weapons

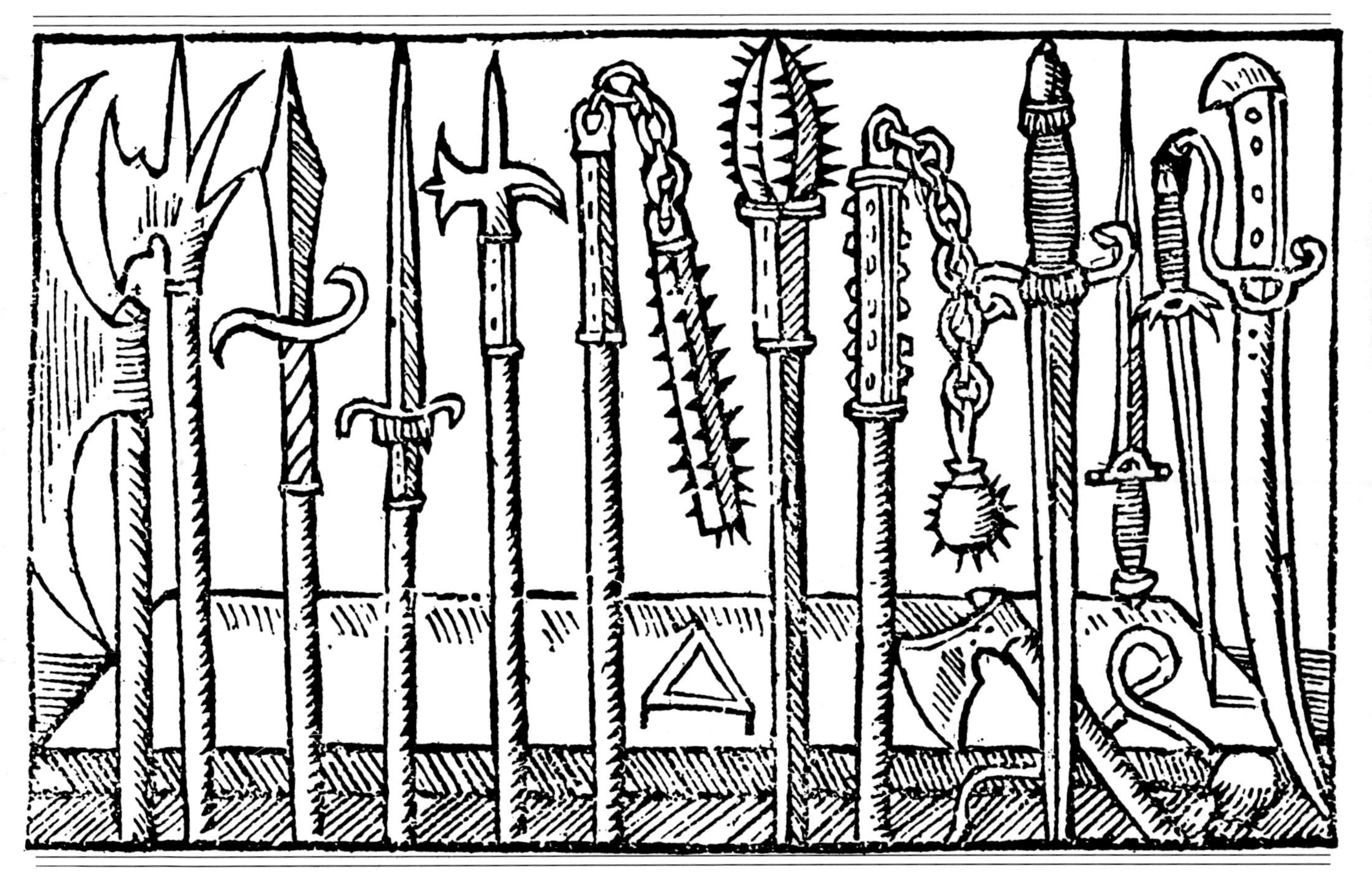

By all accounts, Freydis appeared well-pleased with her wicked doings. She and her men returned to their camp, loaded up the brothers' larger ship with all manner of valuable cargo, and sailed back to Greenland. On the way, Freydis gave clear instructions to her crew. They were to say that the Icelanders had decided to stay on in Vinland. Any man who told the truth of what had happened would be killed by Freydis herself. Having seen Freydis in action, her crew was convinced that she meant what she said.

So the ship sailed into Greenland's Eriksfjord. Freydis sold her cargo, passed out lavish gifts to her crew, then settled down quietly enough on her farm. But it wasn't long before rumors began to leak out about what had really happened in Vinland. When the rumors finally reached Leif Eriksson's ears, he

Eriksfjord

decided to find out the truth. He seized three members of Freydis's crew, tortured them until their confessions matched, then let them go, appalled by the story they told.

The Greenlanders' Saga finishes the tale: "'I have not the heart,' said Leif, 'to punish my sister Freydis as she deserves. But I will predict this of her and her husband: no child of theirs will come to much good.' And such proved the case, that from there on no one thought anything but ill of them."

It's a bleak enough ending to the story of an illustrious family of Greenlanders. Whether or not Freydis's story is true, in whole or in part, she and her brothers were main characters in the discovery and exploration of the North American continent almost a thousand years ago.

Fireweed along Newfoundland's Atlantic coast

Chapter 6
Thorfinn Karlsefni and the First Settlement

Erik the Red's children were not the only Norse explorers to reach North America. One of the most ambitious voyages to the New World was the colonizing expedition led by an Icelandic merchant named Thorfinn Karlsefni.

Thorfinn Karlsefni's story is told in both *Erik the Red's Saga* and *The Greenlanders' Saga*. The two versions don't agree in every detail, and fact and fancy seem to be freely mixed in both. Still, most scholars think that *Erik the Red's Saga* tells Karlsefni's story best. The subtitle of this saga is *Thorfinn Karlsefni's Saga*. Written by Icelanders about Icelanders, the saga was clearly intended to preserve the exploits of a native son as accurately as possible.

According to the saga, Thorfinn Karlsefni "was a man of good family and very well-do-to. . . . He was a trader overseas, and was known to be a good merchant." One of Karlsefni's trading voyages took him to Greenland, where he spent a pleasant winter at Leif Eriksson's home at Brattahlid. Scholars place this visit sometime between the years 1004 and 1020.

While he was at Brattahlid, Karlsefni listened to a lot of exciting talk about Vinland the Good. What he heard convinced him to set out on an expedition himself. But Karlsefni wasn't only interested in exploring or in bringing back rich cargoes. Just as Erik the Red had done in Greenland in 986, Karlsefni wanted to build a colony in Vinland.

Thorfinn Karlsefni set about organizing his trip. He first asked his host if he and his settlers could use Leif's houses at Leifsbudir. Like all others who asked, Karlsefni was told by the prudent Leif that he could borrow the houses, but not have them.

Next Karlsefni assembled his settlers and their supplies. The accounts vary, but he probably set out with three ships, at least 160 men and women, and "all sorts of livestock." One of the women was Karlsefni's new wife, Gudrid. This was the same Gudrid who had first been married to one of the shipwrecked sailors Leif Eriksson had rescued, and who had later married the unlucky Thorstein Eriksson. Now the twice-widowed Gudrid was setting out on her second voyage to Vinland!

When the ships were fitted out, Karlsefni led them northward along Greenland's coast to the Western Settlement. They continued their northward course to Bjarneyjar, or the Bear Isles, which might be today's Holsteinsborg, or possibly Disko Island.

Why did Karlsefni lead his small fleet north and then west, instead of heading due west to begin? Looking at a map, one can see that Karlsefni could have reached Vinland by sailing westward from Greenland to Labrador (which was probably Leif Eriksson's Markland). But that would have meant a sea voyage of some 600 miles (966 kilometers). With a

Rugged glacier in Disko Bay on Greenland's west coast, near the Vikings' Western Settlement

full load of settlers, supplies, and livestock, Karlsefni would have wanted to spend as little time on the open sea, away from fresh food and water, as possible.

Keep in mind that Karlsefni would have been following the recommendations of Leif and the others who had already made the voyage to Vinland. These earlier sailors would have known that Greenland's Bjarneyjar was only 200 miles (322 kilometers) from the easternmost point of Baffin Island (the probable location of Leif Eriksson's Helluland). Clearly, this was the most direct sea route from Greenland to North America.

Remember, too, that Norse sailors could manage north-south, or latitude sailing. But without visible landmarks, they had no reliable way to judge their east-west position, or longitude. A 600-mile westward journey from Brattahlid to Labrador would have been treacherous and fraught with uncertainty. Much safer and more certain was a trip up Greenland's familiar west coast, and then across a mere 200-mile stretch of open sea to Baffin Island and on to Labrador.

So Karlsefni and his ships set out. After an uneventful two days' sailing from Bjarneyjar, they safely reached land. According to *Erik the Red's Saga*, "They rowed ashore in boats and explored the country, finding many flat stones there . . . and many arctic foxes. They gave the land a name, calling it Helluland, or Flatstone Land." Bjarni Herjolfsson, Leif Eriksson,

Arctic fox

Thorfinn Karlsefni—regardless of who actually named Helluland, scholars are certain that all three Norsemen saw the same place, and that place is today's Baffin Island.

From Helluland, "They sailed with a north wind for two days, when land lay ahead of them, with great woods and many wild animals. . . . The land where the forest was they called Markland, Wood Land."

Karlsefni and his ships do not seem to have stopped in Markland. Continuing southward, the saga tells, they came across a cape with the keel from a ship and named the place Kjalarnes, Keelness. Again, it doesn't really matter whether Thorfinn Karlsefni or Thorvald Eriksson named Kjalarnes. It doesn't even matter whether there was, in fact, a real ship's keel on the cape, or whether the name was chosen because the cape itself was shaped like a keel. What is important is that several sources mention the same location in the New World. The evidence suggests that more than one Norseman visited this spot and found it memorable enough to name.

After Kjalarnes, the Norsemen passed long, sandy beaches like those noted in other sagas by Bjarni, Leif, and Thorvald. Karlsefni named these beaches Furdustrandir, meaning Marvelstrands, because it took such a marvelously long time to sail past them.

The Greenlanders' Saga says that Karlsefni and his settlers soon reached Leifsbudir, where they spent two winters living off the bounty of the land. An unfortunate skirmish with natives (the same Skraelings Thorvald encountered?) convinced them to return to Greenland. Before leaving, "they fetched away with them many valuable commodities in the shape of vines, grapes, and furs."

Karlsefni's Scottish slaves bringing grapes and grains

Erik the Red's Saga goes into considerably more detail. In this version, Karlsefni never does find Leifsbudir. Instead, his ships sailed past the Marvelstrands to a shore dotted with bays. Here Karlsefni supposedly sent ashore two Scottish slaves, "fleeter than deer," to scout out the land. When they returned carrying grapes and wild wheat, Karlsefni was pleased, and "said they appeared to have found a choice, fruitful land."

Onward they sailed, until they came to a great fjord. Off the mouth of the fjord was an island they called Straumsey. As the saga tells it, "There were so many birds here that a man could hardly set foot down between the eggs."

Leaving the island, Karlsefni led his ships into the fjord, which they called Straumsfjord. Modern schol-

Gannets nesting at Cape St. Mary's, Newfoundland

ars think it was somewhere along the west coast of Labrador. Here "they carried their goods off the ships and made their preparations. . . . There were mountains there, and the prospect around was beautiful."

Greatly pleased with their new home, the Norse settlers turned their livestock out to graze and spent their time exploring. As long as the warm weather lasted, life in Straumsfjord was easy. But winter, alas, was not far away. As the saga puts it, "a hard winter it proved, with no provision made for it. They were in a bad way for food, and the hunting and fishing failed."

The colonists managed to hold on until spring, when things began to look brighter. Wild game on the mainland, birds' eggs from Straumsey, and ample fish from the sea kept them well fed. And though the humans had a rough winter, the livestock thrived.

With their immediate needs taken care of, Karlsefni and his crew began making plans to find Leif Eriksson's Vinland. Two exploring parties were sent out. Karlsefni himself led the larger party, heading south and east along the coast. A smaller group, consisting of not more than nine men, headed north under the direction of one Thorhall the Hunter.

Now, Thorhall wasn't exactly a popular sort of fellow. He is described in the saga as being tall, dark, and glowering, about middle-aged, sullen and silent as a rule, but underhanded and rude when he did speak. Still, he was known as an excellent hunter, and he was both experienced and fearless when it came to exploring unknown lands.

The seafaring Norsemen were a bold, adventuresome breed.

As a slave, Thorhall probably did not have a very honorable burial. This picture shows a Viking burial at sea, in which the body is set afloat in a flaming vessel.

When he set out with his exploring party, Thorhall was thoroughly disgusted with this quest for Vinland. He had been promised a land of plenty, flowing with wine and rich in natural resources. Instead, he had nearly starved to death during that first difficult winter. Now, as he and his small party of men headed north, they were blown to sea by an unexpected storm. It is possible that they were trying to return to Greenland, and not looking for Leif Eriksson's Vinland at all. In any case, the saga finishes their story by explaining: "They met with a storm and were shipwrecked off Ireland. Here they were badly beaten and made slaves. It was then that Thorhall lost his life."

Thorfinn and Gudrid give thanks on the shores of Hop, believed to be Vinland.

Back in Straumsfjord, Karlsefni and his exploring party set out and sailed south "for a long time, till they reached a river that flowed from the land into a lake and so on to the sea." Naming the place Hop (Landlock Bay), the Norse colonists found good pasturage, forests full of game, wild, self-sown wheat, and plentiful grapes. They also found that "every brook was full of fish. They dug trenches at the point where land and sea met at high tide, and when the tide went out there were halibut in all the trenches."

For two weeks the colonists enjoyed this land of plenty without any disturbances. Then one morning they were surprised to find nine animal-skin canoes

Pastureland at Cape St. Mary's, Newfoundland

sailing up the river toward them. The saga describes the natives, or Skraelings, paddling these canoes as being small and dark, with big eyes and broad cheeks. The two groups stared at each other in mutual astonishment for some time. Then, without a word, the Skraelings canoed down the southern coast.

There were no further excitements that summer. Determined not to be caught unprepared a second time, the colonists busied themselves making houses at Hop for the winter. When winter did come, it was mild, with no snow and easy grazing for the livestock. Though no connection is made in the saga, Karlsefni's Hop sounds remarkably like Leif Eriksson's Vinland.

The Norsemen encounter native people, whom they call Skraelings

The return of spring brought another visit by the Skraelings in their skin boats. This visit turned into a lively trading session. In exchange for beautifully finished furs, the natives seemed happy to receive lengths of Norse red cloth. Scholars are still not sure whether these Skraelings were Inuit or Native American people. In either case, the Norsemen set a pattern for dishonest dealings with a native American population that later European settlers were to continue. As the saga tells it: "Above all these people wanted to buy red cloth . . . and for each fur they got a span's length of cloth, which they tied around their heads. This went on until the Norsemen began to run short of cloth. Then they cut it up so that each length was no more than a finger's width, and yet the Skraelings gave just as much for it, or even more."

The sudden arrival of Karlsefni's bellowing bull put an end to the peaceful scene. The Skraelings, who had never seen such a creature before, paddled off in terror. When they returned some three weeks later, it was to fight, not to trade.

It was a fierce battle. The Norsemen, greatly outnumbered, retreated up the river. When they reached a rocky cliff, they put up a strong resistance. But according to the saga, that's not what saved them.

In a dramatic (and not entirely believable) account, the saga tells how Leif Eriksson's sister Freydis, now pregnant, stopped the Skraeling attack. She dashed into the fray and, using a hastily snatched-up sword, slapped herself on the chest in a warlike frenzy. The Skraelings, appalled by such a sight, fled.

Bold Freydis frightening the Skraelings into a retreat

Did this really happen? *The Greenlanders' Saga* does not mention that Freydis went along on Karlsefni's voyage. And the story as told in *Erik the Red's Saga* certainly sounds as if it were written mostly for dramatic effect. At any rate, the Skraelings did indeed retreat, and Karlsefni and his settlers were saved for the time being. But the battle convinced Karlsefni that, no matter how bountiful this land was, the unfriendly natives would make permanent settlement impossible. He began making plans to return to Greenland.

The colonists first returned to Straumsfjord to prepare their ships for the return journey and fill their holds with cargo. Karlsefni made one last trip in search of Thorhall the Hunter, but all he found was wooded wilderness. By then it was too late in the season to sail to Greenland, so the Norsemen wintered for a third year in Straumsfjord. It was not a happy time. "There was bitter quarreling on account of the women, for the single men who had no women fell foul of the married men who did."

The one bright spot for Karlsefni and his wife, Gudrid, must have been watching their son Snorri grow up. Snorri had been born that first winter in Straumsfjord. His is the first recorded birth of a European child on North American shores. By the time Karlsefni and Gudrid returned to Greenland, Snorri was nearly three years old.

Finally spring arrived. Karlsefni's ship got a south wind easily enough, and before long he and Gudrid and the rest of their boatload arrived safely in Greenland. The second ship, captained by one Bjarni Grimolfsson, wasn't so lucky. The saga reports that his ship soon sailed into "wormy seas." Some of the crew was saved in the lifeboat, but Bjarni himself went down with his ship.

Thus another voyage to Vinland came to a close. Karlsefni's venture seems to have been the first attempt at colonizing the New World. As far as we can tell, the Norsemen felt that Vinland's riches just weren't worth facing the dangers of its unfriendly native population. As *Erik the Red's Saga* put it: "It now seemed clear to Karlsefni that though the quality of the land was admirable, there would always be fear and strife dogging settlers from those who already inhabited it. So they made ready to leave, setting their hearts on their own country."

It would be another five hundred years before Christopher Columbus's "discovery" of America would lead to European colonization of the New World.

Christopher Columbus in the New World. He was hailed at the time as the first European to set foot on American soil.

Chapter 7
Sagas and Sources

The Norse exploration of North America took place some thousand years ago. The adventurers who reached Helluland, Markland, Vinland, Straumsfjord, and Hop—and Iceland and Greenland before that—left no maps or guidebooks about what they saw. How, then, have the stories of their explorations been preserved for so many years?

First of all, the stories survived the way most good stories do—they were told and retold to interested listeners. For hundreds of years, tales of intrepid Norse men and women—Naddod the Viking, Erik the Red, Leif Eriksson, Thorfinn Karlsefni, and the bloodthirsty Freydis—were told around the hearth fires of Greenland, Iceland, and Norway. Because these stories held the history of the Norse people, the tellers were careful to repeat the stories accurately and to include a wealth of detail.

In cultures all over the world, oral storytelling has been both an entertainment and a fine art.

Frequently, the stories were told in the form of poetry. It was easier for a storyteller to remember the fixed phrases and rhythmic patterns of a poem than the more loosely arranged words of a prose story. From generation to generation, the same stories and poems were passed down, word for word.

Eventually, people began to write down these stories and poems. By the twelfth and thirteenth centuries, Norse oral storytelling was rapidly being replaced by written sagas and epic poems. More often than not, the authors of these sagas and epics were from Iceland.

What exactly is a saga? The word itself simply means something said, or something recorded in words. Icelandic sagas are prose stories that tell the histories of medieval Icelandic families and Norwegian kings. Most Icelandic sagas are rather bloody tales, dealing mainly with insults and feuds, killings and counter-killings. Many of these sagas were written as family histories. They preserved the pride and reputations of families living on an isolated island far from the rest of civilized Europe.

The Icelanders' long winter nights provided ample time for weaving words into stories. When Christianity introduced books and the Latin alphabet to the island, the Icelanders found they were naturals in the art of written literature.

Replica of a Viking family at L'Anse aux Meadows

Greenlanders and Icelanders dry their fish on racks today, just as they have for centuries.

Oddly enough, the Icelanders' farming practices also helped them become writers. Their rocky, mountainous island couldn't support many crops, but it did have pastures for grazing animals. So most Icelanders lived by raising cows, sheep, horses, pigs, goats, and geese. Iceland's pastures, however, were covered with snow for much of the year. Rather than feed livestock through the long, dark winter, Icelandic farmers killed many of their animals in the fall. They then salted or dried the meat for eating and scraped and treated the hides to make vellum. And fine, smooth vellum was what people wrote on in those days.

Icelanders had a vast array of subjects to write about. They produced the Poetic Edda, a collection of poems about Norse gods and heroes, and the Prose Edda. In the *Heimskringla*, they recorded stories of the lives of Norway's kings. The *Landnamabok* and the *Islendingabok* record the history and settlement of Iceland (and its Greenland colony), while family sagas like *Greenlanders' Saga* and *Erik the Red's Saga* recast this history in a more imaginative vein.

Energetic and intelligent, Icelandic writers were also known far and wide for translating and adapting foreign works. As the Danish historian Saxo Grammaticus wrote (before he coolly copied from Icelandic sources!): "The diligence of the men of Iceland must not be shrouded in silence; since the barrenness of their native soil offers no means of self-indulgence, they pursue a steady routine of temperance and devote all their time to improving our knowledge of others' deeds, compensating for poverty by their intelligence. They regard it a real pleasure to discover and commemorate the achievements of every nation; in their judgement it is as elevating to discourse on the

Reproduction of a carving found in Sweden, showing scenes from a Norse saga

prowess of others as to display their own. Thus I have . . . composed a considerable part of this present work by copying their narratives, not scorning where I recognized such skill in ancient lore to take these men as witness."

Unfortunately, the vast majority of original Icelandic writings have been lost over the centuries. Some were destroyed by fires and floods. Others were eaten away by mice, worms, and insects. One collection went down in a tragic shipwreck in 1682; another was lost in the great Copenhagen (Denmark) fire of 1728. Saddest of all are the many priceless manuscripts that were converted by their poverty-stricken owners into shoes and clothing. One of the most touching displays in the Icelandic National Museum is a vellum manuscript cut in the shape of half a man's vest, complete with stitch marks and buttonholes.

Still, enough of the writings have survived to show modern readers their greatness. Among these are the sagas that tell the story of the Norse discovery and colonization of Greenland and America, or Vinland.

But should these sagas be regarded as truth? Saga writers, as serious historians, would naturally value accuracy. But as artists hoping to hold their readers' interest, they would just as naturally value creative imagination in shaping a story.

Then, too, a written saga could only be as historically accurate as its source. In writing stories that had been told orally for generations, saga writers were forced to rely on the memories and recitation abilities of oral storytellers. Certainly, some details would be lost in the mists of time. Just as certainly, other details might be added, to provide a missing motive or a bit of snappy dialogue.

4,000-year-old stone carvings near Sarpsborg, southern Norway

The fact remains that, no matter how disciplined and responsible their authors were, the sagas were written some two hundred to four hundred years after the events they narrated took place. When we read that Bjarni Herjolfsson said, "Our voyage will seem foolhardy, since none of us here has ever sailed the Greenland Sea," we are hearing a conversation that supposedly took place hundreds of years before it was ever written down. Did Bjarni really say those exact words? The saga says he did, but we have no way of knowing for sure. The best we can assume is that Bjarni was the kind of man who *might* have said them. Likewise, Erik the Red was the kind of man who might, in his turn, have said, "It is not my destiny to discover any more lands," or Tyrkir the German might have excitedly exclaimed, "I have found vines and grapes!"

Map drawn by Sigurd Stephanius in 1570, possibly using ancient Icelandic sagas as a guide. He identifies point A as Vinland.

Besides word-for-word conversations, modern readers must question other aspects of the sagas. Sometimes the stories contain elements that seem sheer fantasy. In one version of Thorfinn Karlsefni's voyage, Thorvald Eriksson is killed by a mysterious one-legged creature called a Uniped. (Never mind that in another version he has already been killed!) Scholars have identified this Uniped as everything from a hopping Inuit native to a limping polar bear. But the most likely explanation is that the Uniped was a folkloric monster familiar to twelfth- and thirteenth-century Icelandic writers.

This bring up another issue: Even when different versions of a story agree in general, they vary widely in their details. All we know about the Greenland and

Because early seafarers faced the terrors of the unknown, their imaginations went wild.

Vinland adventures comes from two sagas, *The Greenlanders' Saga* and *Erik the Red's Saga*. But the two sagas don't tell the same story. The characters, plots, and sequence of events in each are quite different. How can this be?

The answer lies in why each saga was written. *The Greenlanders' Saga* is the history of Erik the Red's children. It was written about a prominent Greenland family and its exploits. Erik's own discovery and settlement of Greenland is treated but briefly. The main thrust of the saga is the Eriksson children's adventures in Vinland.

Erik the Red's Saga, on the other hand, tells the story from the Icelandic point of view. Erik was himself a native Icelander. In this saga, his discovery and settlement of Greenland—Iceland's only colony—is given much more emphasis. Leif's discovery of Vinland rates a mere paragraph of text. Even when the two versions agree in general, they vary widely in details.

Most scholars agree that *The Greenlanders' Saga* offers the most accurate information about the Eriksson family voyages. But even so, other sagas still provide a wealth of information about medieval Norse explorations. The essential facts of the sagas and family histories remain undisputed: Over a period of some three hundred years, Norse adventurers systematically pushed back the western boundaries of the known world. From Norway to Iceland, from Iceland to Greenland, and from Greenland on to America, the surge of Norse seamen moved ever westward. We may never know exactly which Norseman discovered which new land at which precise moment in time. But we know they were here.

And the sagas are not our only evidence!

Chapter 8
The Proof Is in the Digging

For years, scholars argued about whether or not Leif Eriksson and the Vikings did in fact beat Christopher Columbus to America. Besides the sagas, medieval literature contains just a few passing references to lands west of Greenland. Adam of Bremen, an eleventh-century German historian, wrote: "There is an island in that ocean visited by many, which is called Vinland, for the reason that vines grow wild there, which yield the best of wine. Moreover, unsown grain grows there in abundance, and this we know is not a fabulous fancy, for the accounts of the Danes prove that it is a fact."

Vinland is also mentioned briefly in the *Islendingabok*, the history of Iceland written about 1122, and in various other Icelandic histories. Vinland appears in early Catholic Church communications, as home to a possible lost colony of faithfuls in need of spiritual guidance. Then, after about the fourteenth century, references to Vinland disappear from written records. In time, Vinland was forgotten. The Norse discovery of America was lost in the excitement of Christopher Columbus's historic journey in 1492.

Well, perhaps not entirely lost. Readers of Icelandic literature still had the sagas. Throughout the ages, there were always scholars who clung stubbornly to the belief that the sagas were basically true. In the mid-nineteenth century, the arguments of several such scholars inspired Americans to comb their eastern seaboard for artifacts left by early Norse visitors. As a result, artifacts by the dozen were turned up—but none was judged genuine.

Then, in 1880, a Viking warship dating from the mid-ninth century was discovered in Gokstad, Norway. That such a ship could indeed sail across the Atlantic Ocean was proved in 1893, when a seaman named Magnus Andersen sailed an exact replica of it from Norway to Newfoundland.

Reconstruction of the Norse ship discovered at Gokstad, Norway, in 1880

Once it was proven the Norsemen *could* have sailed to North America, interest in how and where and when grew stronger. Scholars went back to the sagas to try to figure out just where Leif Eriksson and his fellow seamen had sailed. But the vague descriptions of shorelines and forests, rivers and mountains, led to never-ending arguments. Were those really glaciers Leif Eriksson saw on Markland, or just snow-capped mountains? When Thorfinn Karlsefni sailed "two days"

Rocky Baffin Island, believed to be Eriksson's Helluland

from Markland to Vinland, how many miles did he travel? What about the "self-sown grain" they both reported finding? Was that a true grain, such as rye or wheat, or a kind of wild rice? This is important, because the two grow in different places in North America.

Today, the debate has calmed down somewhat, and most scholars agree on the locations identified in the sagas. Helluland, with its glaciered mountains, flat, stony coastline, and abundance of Arctic foxes is most probably Baffin Island, in the Canadian Arctic. The keel-shaped cape (Kjalarnes), long, sandy beaches (Marvelstrands), and dense forests of Markland sound remarkably like Cape Porcupine and The Strand on the coast of Labrador.

But where was Leif Eriksson's Vinland? For a century, various guesses placed it as far north as Labrador, and as far south as Cape Cod, Massachusetts. Some people insisted the Norsemen made it inland all the way to Minnesota and Oklahoma, while others had them sailing happily into Maryland's Chesapeake Bay. Sailing south from Labrador, the next logical landing point is northern Newfoundland. Great Sacred Island off Newfoundland's northern tip could well be the island with the sweet-tasting dew mentioned in *The Greenlanders' Saga*. The nearby Strait of Belle Isle could be Leif's channel flowing between the isle and the mainland. There are the pasturelands Leif mentioned, and all the salmon one could want swimming up Black Duck Brook to their spawning grounds.

A modern-day view of the Strait of Belle Isle

Brook at L'Anse aux Meadows where the Vikings are thought to have fished for salmon

Then, in 1960, an archaeological team headed by the Norwegian husband-and-wife team of Helge Ingstad and Anne Stine positively identified the remains of a medieval Norse settlement at this very point. It was an exciting moment. After years of diligent searching, Ingstad and Stine had found actual physical proof that Norsemen had indeed landed on American shores!

For the next eight years, Anne Stine supervised a thorough excavation of the site. More excavations followed, and in 1977, L'Anse aux Meadows (the site takes its name from the nearest village) became a Canadian National Historic Park. The site was opened to the public and a visitors' display center established.

Reconstructed Norse settlement at L'Anse aux Meadows

Viking sod dwelling at the L'Anse aux Meadows site

What did archaeologists find at L'Anse aux Meadows? There were the remains of at least eight Norse buildings, constructed of sod and wood and built in a traditional Icelandic-Greenland style. Three of them appeared to be living quarters, with fireplaces running down the center and wooden sleeping bunks or seating platforms along the walls.

Workshops, storage rooms, and a forge made up the rest of the buildings. From the many pieces of worked wood and iron rivets found, it appears that the workshops were used mainly for repairing and rebuilding boats. Some of the smaller workshops were apparently used for cooking and as smokehouses. A forge for smelting the local bog iron was also found, along with a charcoal-pit kiln.

Most of the artifacts found were the sorts of things men would use to repair ships and fishing lines and to

Replicas of Norse buildings at L'Anse aux Meadows Historic Park

make new tools. A few sewing needles and knitting spindles were the only clues that women had ever stayed at L'Anse aux Meadows.

L'Anse aux Meadows seems to have been a Norse camp occupied for a relatively short time. There were enough sleeping bunks to accommodate as many as eighty-five people at any one time. The absence of burial grounds or large garbage heaps suggests that humans didn't live here for very long. Since there were no barns or other evidence of animals at the settlement, it was probably never meant to be a permanent farming colony. Finally, sod buildings such as those at L'Anse aux Meadows would have to be replaced every twenty years or so in Newfoundland's damp climate. But there is no evidence that the original buildings were ever rebuilt. This, too, suggests that no one lived here for long.

Decorative segment of a spindle found at L'Anse aux Meadows

Over the years, archaeologists and other scientists—biologists, geologists, chemists, botanists, oceanographers, and physicists—have run all kinds of tests on the artifacts found at L'Anse aux Meadows. They have also tested plant, soil, and water samples taken from the site. The results indicate that people did indeed once live there, sometime between the last years of the tenth and the first half of the eleventh century. The buildings and artifacts, combined with the sagas, point without a doubt to Norse explorers such as Leif Eriksson and Thorfinn Karlsefni.

Viking stone lamp excavated at the L'Anse aux Meadows site

Charles C. Rafn, a nineteenth-century Norse-saga scholar, drew this map believing that Vinland was on the coast of Massachusetts.

But was L'Anse aux Meadows really Vinland? True, it has meadows and a river, an island and a current, and, perhaps most importantly, it has the remnants of authentic Norse living quarters. The only thing it doesn't have is—grapevines.

Grapevines have been the problem ever since people really started believing in Leif Eriksson and his fellow explorers. Why? Because grapes just don't grow as far north as Newfoundland. They might survive as far north as southern Nova Scotia. But they only become abundant much farther south, in New England. That's why for so many years people believed New England, and Cape Cod in particular, was the site of Leif Eriksson's Vinland.

Were Vinland's "grapes" really cranberries?

Grapes were one of the main reasons for the Norse excitement over the New World. The name itself, Vinland, promises grapes and wine in abundance. Some scholars argue that the Norse "grapes" were really currants or cranberries or gooseberries, any of which could be used to make a sort of wine. Others suggest that Leif made exaggerated claims about his new-found land. Just as his father chose the name "Greenland" to appeal to land-hungry settlers, Leif could have picked "Vinland" to appeal to colonists. Still other scholars have suggested that Vinland really comes from the Old Norse word for "grassland" rather than "wineland." Certainly pasturage was important for Norse farmers—but how, then, can we explain the specific discussions of wine that appear in the sagas and elsewhere?

Finally, some scholars have pointed out that weather and growing conditions could well have been different a thousand years ago. When Jacques Cartier discovered Canada's Saint Lawrence River in the 1530s, he reported grapes growing abundantly on both the north and the south sides of the river. Perhaps grapes really *did* grow in Newfoundland at the time of the Norse explorations.

We may never know the whole truth of the matter. Perhaps L'Anse aux Meadows was just one of several Norse camps in North America. It may have been Vinland, or Hop, or Straumsfjord, or none of these.

Perhaps someday, archaeologists will unearth evidence that solves these mysteries. Until that day, we still have L'Anse aux Meadows. And with L'Anse aux Meadows we have the proof that the Norse exploration of America wasn't just a fiction. The Norsemen were here.

Explorer Jacques Cartier sets up a cross at Gaspe, southwest of the Vinland site, about five hundred years after the Viking settlement. Cartier reported seeing grapes when he was there.

Chapter 9
After Vinland

L'Anse aux Meadows proves that medieval Norse seamen did indeed reach the Atlantic shores of North America. The question that remains is whether they also explored other regions in America. Over the years, dozens of claims have been made about Norse artifacts found around the country.

For years the famous Stone Tower in Newport, Rhode Island, was believed to be a medieval Norse structure. Archaeological studies, however, have shown that it was built around 1675 by Benedict Arnold, then governor of Rhode Island. Nevertheless, some people would still like to believe it was built by Leif Eriksson or his fellow Norsemen.

A replica of the Kensington runestone, found on the farm of Olaf Ohman in 1898. It tells of a tragic Viking voyage that supposedly took place in 1362.

Even more famous was the Kensington Stone, whose origins are still hotly debated. In 1898, a Swedish-born farmer in Kensington, Minnesota, claimed to have found a 200-pound (91-kilogram) stone bearing a type of writing known as runes. For years scholars debated about the stone, ran tests on it, and theorized how Norse explorers could have made their way so far inland. Eventually, most scholars agreed the Kensington Stone was a fake, but even today there are some who insist that it is genuine.

The old Stone Tower, or Stone Mill, in Newport, Rhode Island

Another stone with rune-like inscriptions was found at Heavener in the Poteau Mountains of southeastern

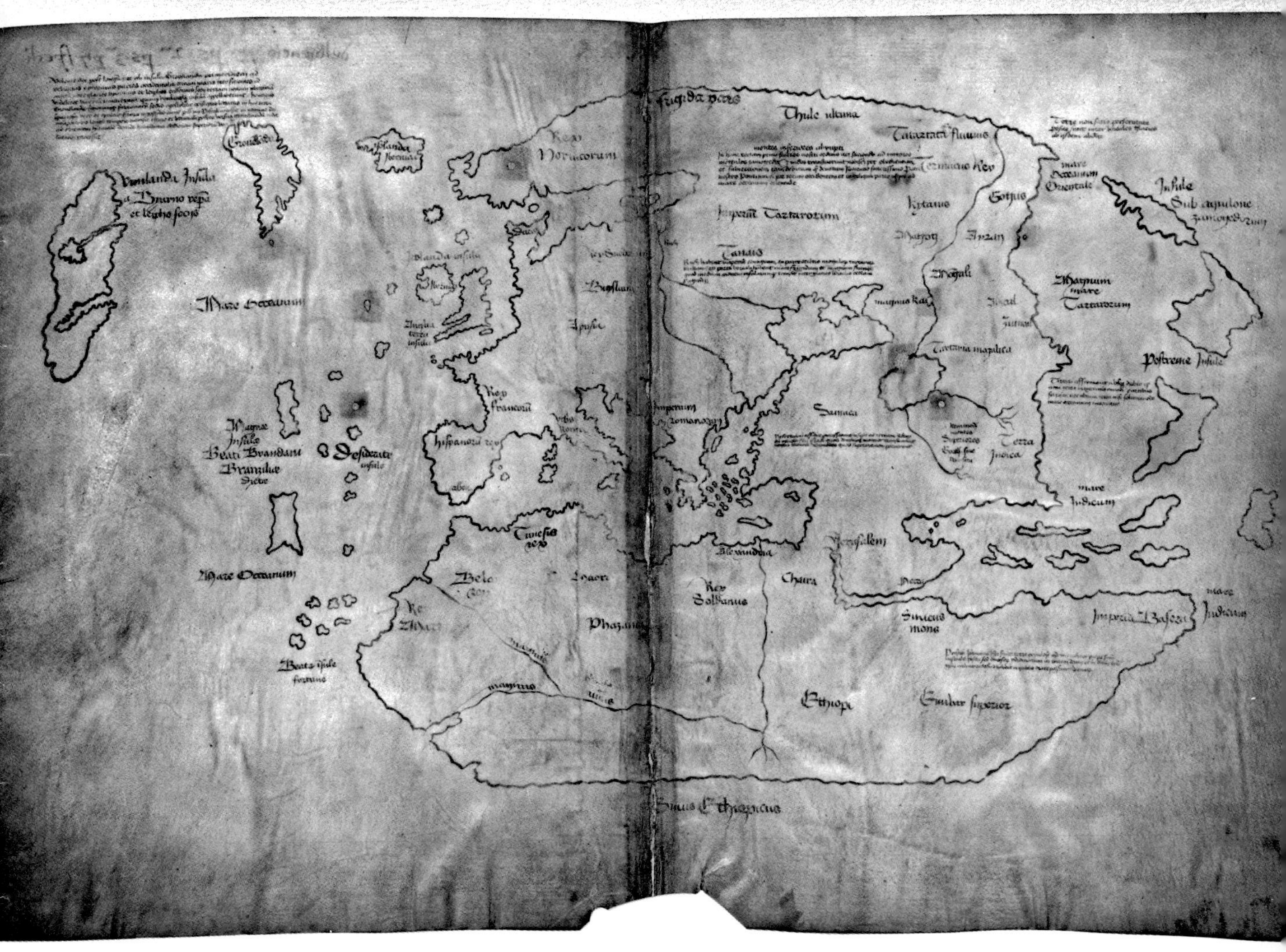

The famous "Vinland map"

Oklahoma. Like so many other Norse "artifacts," the Heavener runestone is believed to be a hoax—though there are still people fighting to have it recognized as genuine.

Probably the most famous and most controversial piece of "evidence" that Norse adventurers discovered North America is the Vinland Map. Unveiled by Yale University in 1965, the map was said to date from A.D. 1440. This would make it the only map to include Vinland before Columbus's discovery. But, like so many other artifacts, the Vinland Map is today generally accepted as a hoax.

And so the search goes on. Future archaeological digs may uncover additional evidence of Norsemen's presence in America. Until they do, we will have to be satisfied knowing that, some five hundred years before Columbus, Norsemen reached American shores. The Norse discovery of America wasn't an accidental, isolated incident. Rather, it was one of a series of deliberately planned westward advances. Using their knowledge of seamanship and sea lore, adventure-loving Norse sailors moved from Norway to the North Atlantic islands, to Iceland, to Greenland, and then, finally, to America.

From the sagas and the archaeological finds, it seems clear that the Norsemen intended to settle in the new lands they found across the western ocean. They brought with them their families and livestock and whole boatloads of supplies. But when they met with unfriendly natives, they began to reconsider. Vinland had much to offer in the way of natural resources. But everything else the settlers would need—ready-made tools and clothing, shipbuilding materials, grain, salt, spices, and luxury items—would have to come from Greenland, via Iceland, via Norway. The stepping stones across the Atlantic were leading farther and farther from the family, friends, and security of their homeland. The time just wasn't right for a permanent settlement in this new land, and the Norsemen returned home.

Thorfinn Karlsefni and Gudrid eventually settled in Thorfinn's native Iceland, where they lived long and illustrious lives. After Thorfinn's death, Gudrid turned to religion. She made several pilgrimages to Rome, Italy, and is recorded in Icelandic annals as having a long line of bishops among her descendants.

A bay on the coast of Labrador, which is believed to be Leif Eriksson's Markland. Eriksson described Markland as flat and wooded, with beaches running up to the forest.

Back in Greenland, Leif Eriksson assumed his father's role as the island's most prominent citizen. The rest of his family didn't fare so well. Thorvald had died in Vinland and Thorstein in the Western Settlement, and, as it was written, "no one thought anything but ill" of Freydis.

Gradually, Vinland became little more than a distant dream. There is some evidence that timber-gathering expeditions to Markland continued for some years, but no one made any further attempts at colonizing the new lands. Vinland's short chapter in a long saga had ended.

Unbeknownst to Leif Eriksson, Greenland's chapter in the saga was doomed to end soon, too. Tragically, over the next several hundred years, both the Eastern and Western settlements would die of neglect. The weather grew colder, the drift ice around the island grew denser, and the supply ships from Iceland—itself racked by plagues, famines, earthquakes, and volcanoes—stopped coming. Unable to save even themselves, the Greenlanders could never have supported an American colony.

Viking ruins at Julianehaad Fjord, Greenland, dating from the early 1400s

Viking raiders in a "dragon ship"

No one knows exactly how or when or why the last Greenlander died. Late in the summer of 1410, visitors from Iceland attended a Greenland wedding and waved good-bye as they sailed back home. It was the last anyone was to hear from the island. After that, all was silence.

By the year 1492, European attention was directed toward an Italian sailor named Christopher Columbus and the new lands he had discovered across the Atlantic Ocean.

But the ships from the north had been there first.

Appendices

Codex Annal. Reg. no. 2087.

1\. [illegible]

2\. [illegible]

Codex Arna Magn. no. 420 in 4to Annal. Skalholt. vetustorum.

3\. [illegible]

1. Bishop Eric's voyage to Vineland in the year 1121.
2. Discovery made by the Iceland clergymen Addalbrand and Thorwald Helgason in the year 1285.
3. A voyage to Markland (Nova Scotia) in the year 1347.

Chas. C. Rafn.

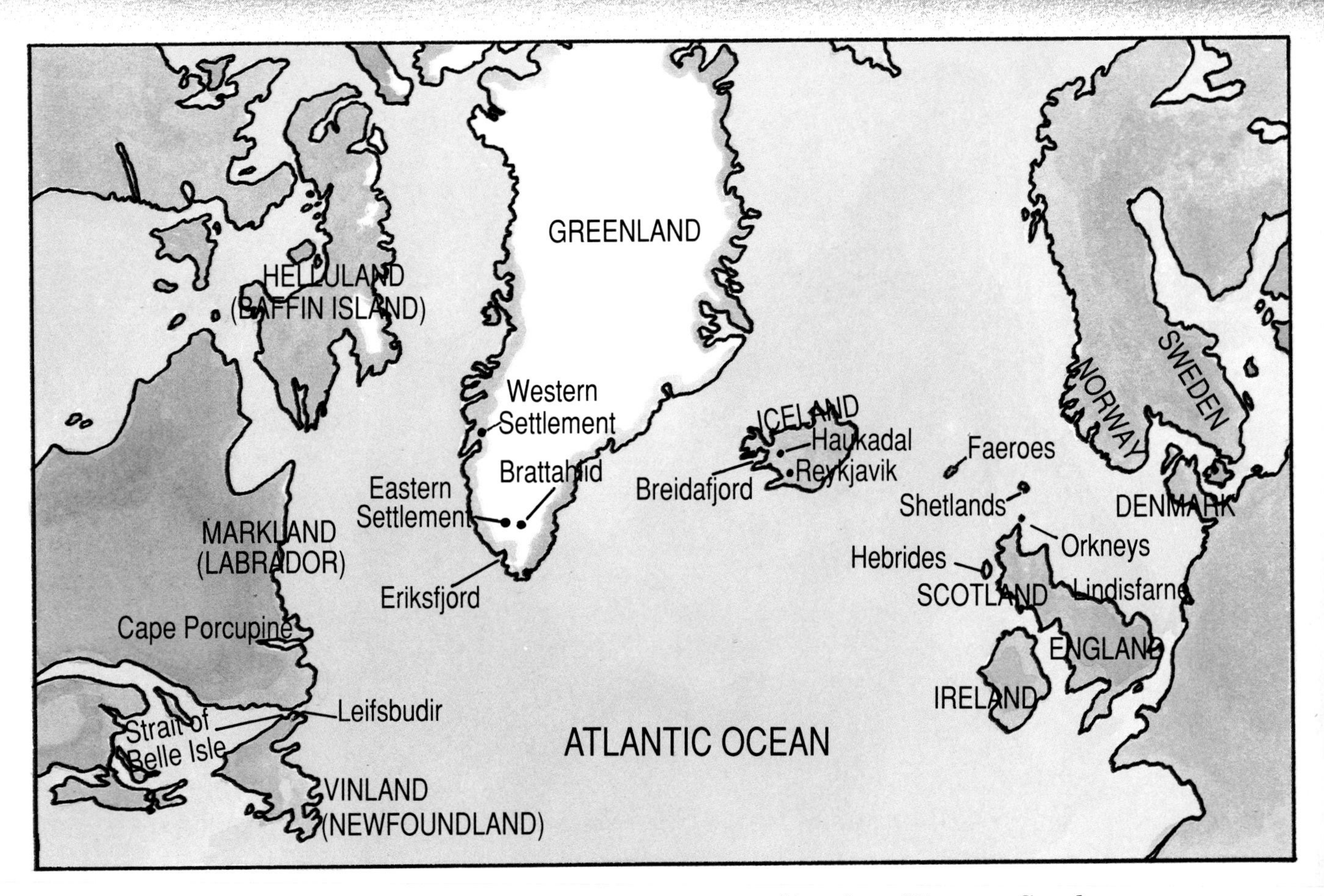

Around the year A.D. 800, Vikings began spreading from Norway, Sweden, and Denmark into continental Europe, the British Isles, and other islands in the North Atlantic Ocean. Norsemen continued pushing west, settling in Iceland in the 870s. Icelandic settler Erik the Red moved on to Greenland and brought settlers there in 986. In 1001, Erik's son Leif sailed still farther west, reaching Baffin Island, Labrador, and Newfoundland.

Opposite page:
Items 1, 2, and 3 at the top of this picture are portions of Norse sagas. They are reprinted in the *Antiquitates Americanae* of Danish historian Charles C. Rafn (1795-1864). Between and beneath the inscriptions, Rafn has written notes to explain them. Rafn, who published his book in 1837, believed that Markland was Nova Scotia and Vinland was on the coast of Massachusetts. For many years, Norse scholars shared his views. Today, however, it is more certain that these settlements were farther north and that Markland was Labrador and Vinland was on the coast of Newfoundland.

Timeline of Viking Explorations

793—Vikings attack and pillage the northern English monastery of Lindisfarne

Mid-800s—Vikings have spread from Norway into the Shetland, Orkney, Hebrides, and Faeroe islands of the North Atlantic Ocean

About 860—Gardar, sailing for the Hebrides, is blown off course to Iceland; he spends a winter there and names it Gardarsholm; later, Naddod the Viking accidentally finds the same island and names it Snaeland

860s—The Viking Floki Vilgerdarson sails to Iceland, spends a winter there, and names the island Iceland

870s—Viking settlers begin moving to Iceland

875—Ingolf the Viking builds a home at Reykjavik, Iceland

Between 900 and 930—Gunnbjorn Ulf-Krakuson's ship is blown westward from Iceland, and he sights new lands ("Gunnbjorn's Skerries") to the west

930—Icelandic Vikings meet in their first *Althing*, an assembly to make laws and settle disputes

About 960—Thorvald, Leif Eriksson's grandfather, settles in Iceland

982—Erik the Red, expelled from Iceland, sets sail to find Gunnbjorn's Skerries; he discovers a large island, which he names Greenland

986—Several shiploads of Icelanders sail to Greenland to establish a colony; merchant Bjarni Herjolfsson, sailing from Iceland to Greenland, is blown off course to the southwest and sights new lands

1001—Leif Eriksson, Eric the Red's son, sails westward from the Greenland colony to find the land described by Bjarni Herjolfsson; he sails to Baffin Island, naming it Helluland; to Labrador, naming it Markland; and to Newfoundland, naming it Vinland

1002—Leif's brother Thorvald sails to Labrador, winters there, and is mortally wounded in a battle with Skraelings (North American natives)

Between 1004 and 1020— On a trading voyage, Thorfinn Karlsefni goes to Greenland, spending the winter at Leif Eriksson's home at Brattahlid

1009—Thorfinn Karlsefni brings settlers from Greenland to Vinland

1013—Karlsefni and his colonists leave Vinland; later, Leif Eriksson's sister, Freydis, sails to Vinland, where she tricks and kills her partners

Late 1000s—German historian Adam of Bremen mentions Vinland in his writings

1100s to 1200s—The Norse tradition of oral storytelling is replaced by a written tradition of historical sagas and epic poems

About 1122—Vinland is mentioned in the *Islendingabok*, a history of Iceland

1200s— Norwegian guidebook called *The King's Mirror* describes colonial Greenland

1410—Icelanders visit Greenland for a wedding; this is the last time the Greenland colonists are ever seen

1880—A Viking warship dating from the mid-800s is discovered in Norway

1893—Magnus Andersen sails a replica of a Viking ship from Norway to Newfoundland, proving that such a ship could sail across the Atlantic Ocean

1960—Near L'Anse aux Meadows on Great Sacred Island off Newfoundland's northern tip, Norwegian archaeologists Helge Ingstad and Anne Stine discover ruins of a medieval Norse settlement, dating from the late-tenth to early-eleventh century

Glossary of Terms

astrolabe—An instrument used by seamen to calculate the position of celestial bodies

azimuth—The path of a star in its regular arc through the sky

balmy—Mild, soothing

blithely—Cheerfully or carelessly

broadsword—A sword with a wide blade

concentric—Having the same center

disgruntled—Out of sorts

exiled—Sent away by force and forbidden to return

exploits—Daring deeds

falcon—A bird of prey, sometimes trained for sport

fjord—A narrow inlet between steep cliffs

foster-brother—An adopted brother

gale—A fierce storm

glacier—A mountain-like river of ice

habitable—Able to be lived in

heathen—Someone with no religious beliefs

hermit—Someone who lives alone, far from civilization

hoax—A forgery or trick

homestead—A tract of land where someone settles down and makes a home

inheritance—Money, goods, or land received from relatives after their death

inhospitable—Unfriendly; providing no food or shelter

intrepid—Bold, daring, fearless

kiln—A furnace for hardening pottery

latitude—One's position in terms of north and south

legitimate—Proper, lawful

longitude—One's position in terms of east and west

longship—A swift, low-sided Viking warship

marauders—Raiders

medieval—A period in European history from about A.D. 500 to 1500, also known as the Middle Ages

pasturage—Land where cattle can graze

persuasive—Able to convince or persuade

plunder—To overrun, destroy, and take goods during wartime

prow—The front point of a boat, often having a decorative carving

runes—A type of writing used by medieval Germanic people

ruthless—Lacking mercy or kindness

sagas—Stories, most written by Icelanders, about Norse kings, Icelandic families, and their deeds

sod—Soil matted with grass and roots

starboard—The right side of a boat

terrain—Landscape

thrall—A slave

truce—A peace agreement

vellum—The skin of a lamb or calf, used as a writing material

Bibliography

For further reading, see:

Atkinson, Ian. *The Viking Ships*. NY: Cambridge University Press/Lerner Publications, 1980.

Clarke, Helen. *Vikings*. NY: Gloucester Press, 1979.

Crossley-Holland, Kevin, editor. *The Faber Book of Northern Legends*. Winchester, MA: Faber & Faber, 1983.

Ferguson, Sheila. *Growing Up in Viking Times*. London: Ratsford Academic and Educational Limited, 1981.

Golding, Morton J. *The Mystery of the Vikings in America*. NY: Lippincott, 1973.

Grant, Neil. *Explorers*. Morristown, NJ: Silver Burdett, 1982.

Haugaard, Erik C. *Leif the Unlucky*. Boston: Houghton Mifflin, 1982.

Hintz, Martin. *Norway*. Chicago: Childrens Press, 1982.

Lepthien, Emilie. *Greenland*. Chicago: Childrens Press, 1989.

Lepthien, Emilie. *Iceland*. Chicago: Childrens Press, 1987.

Martell, Hazel. *The Vikings*. NY: Warwick Press, 1986.

Index

Page numbers in boldface type indicate illustrations.

Picture Identifications for Chapter Opening Spreads

6-7—Wild grapes
20-21—Norse raid under Olaf Tryggvason
28-29—View across the bay from Reykjavik, Iceland
44-45—View along the Icelandic coast
56-57—Polar bears and parhelia (mock suns), Greenland
72-73—Baffin Island, Eriksson's Helluland
88-89—Snow-covered trees in Norway
98-99—Foundations of Viking buildings at L'Anse aux Meadows
110-111—Field of wildflowers, eastern Canada

Acknowledgment

For a critical reading of the manuscript, our thanks to John Parker, Ph.D., Curator, James Ford Bell Library, University of Minnesota, Minneapolis, Minnesota

Picture Acknowledgments

© Cameramann International, Ltd.—112 (top)

© Joan Dunlop—40, 71, 98-99, 102, 103 (2 pictures)

Historical Pictures Service—11, 13, 20-21, 26, 36, 38, 47, 64, 81, 87, 109

Journalism Services—22, 84, 117

© Emilie Lepthien—12, 41, 44-45, 49, 52, 54, 55, 59, 68, 70, 92

North Wind Picture Archives—9, 16, 17, 23, 24, 25, 27, 32, 37, 43, 51 (3 pictures), 61, 65, 69, 78, 80, 82, 85, 90, 93, 95, 96, 100, 107, 115, 118; © Jim Scourletis—112 (margin)

Photri: 5; © Andrews-Orange–79

© Bob and Ira Spring—2, 35, 94

SuperStock International, Inc.—4, 116

TSW-Click/Chicago, Ltd.: 88-89; © George Hunter—19, 75; © Ian Walker—28-29; © Kenneth Alden—31

Valan: © Harold V. Green—6-7; © G. Van Ryckevorsel—15; © Gerhard Kahrmann—18; © Johnny Johnson—53; © Fred Bruemmer—56-57, 58, 63, 76; © Francis Lepine—62, 104 (bottom); © S. J. Krasemann—72-73, 108; © J. Hugessen—83; © Jane K. Hugessen—91, 104 (margin), 105, 106; © Pam Hickman—101; © Jean Bruneau—110-111

Yale University Library—113

Map by Len Meents—119

Cover illustration by Steven Gaston Dobson

About the Author

Charnan Simon grew up in Ohio, Georgia, Oregon, and Washington State. She holds a B.A. degree in English Literature from Carleton College in Northfield, Minnesota, and an M.A. in English Literature from the University of Chicago. She worked for children's trade book companies after college and became the managing editor of *Cricket* magazine before beginning her career as a free-lance writer. Ms. Simon has written dozens of books and articles for young people and especially likes writing—and reading—history, biography, and fiction of all sorts. She lives in Chicago with her husband and two daughters.